AMERICAN RACISM:

Exploration of the Nature of Prejudice

AMERICAN RACISM:

Exploration of
the Nature of Prejudice

ROGER DANIELS

The University of Wyoming

HARRY H. L. KITANO

University of California, Los Angeles

PRENTICE-HALL, INC.

Englewood Cliffs, New Jersey

PRENTICE-HALL INTERNATIONAL, INC., *London*
PRENTICE-HALL OF AUSTRALIA, PTY. LTD., *Sydney*
PRENTICE-HALL OF CANADA, LTD., *Toronto*
PRENTICE-HALL OF INDIA PRIVATE LTD., *New Delhi*
PRENTICE-HALL OF JAPAN, INC., *Tokyo*

Current printing (last digit):
10 9 8 7 6 5 4 3 2 1

C-13-029009-2

P-13-028993-0

Library of Congress Catalog Card Number: 73-87261

Printed in the United States of America

For Our Children—
May They Grow Up in
a Less Racist America

A State which is incompetent to satisfy different races condemns itself; a State which labors to neutralise, to absorb, or to expel them, destroys its own vitality; a State which does not include them is destitute of the chief basis of self-government.

LORD ACTON, 1862.

Preface

"The problem of the 20th century," wrote W. E. B. Du Bois seventy years ago, "is the problem of the color line—the relation of the darker to the lighter races of men in Asia and Africa, in America and the islands of the sea." Like so many sibylline statements, this one said too much and too little: there have been other twentieth-century problems and the color line, as Du Bois well knew, went back several centuries. Yet, all in all, his was a perceptive insight, particularly when one considers the accommodationist atmosphere which permeated the thought of other turn-of-the-century intellectuals, white and black. In the past seven decades, the startling relevance of the color line to the basic problems of American democracy has become more and more apparent. The literature of race relations is enormous and growing at what seems like a geometric ratio. How then can we justify yet another book?

The answer to that question, we hope, will be obvious to most of our readers. In the first instance, we approach the problem from a unique angle; each of us has been concerned previously with what is, at least numerically, a minor phase of American racism—discrimination against yellow men rather than black. And for one of the authors, involvement with this question has been more than academic. A second-generation Japanese American (or Nisei),

Kitano was "relocated" along with the rest of the West Coast Japanese and enjoyed the relatively rare privilege of being graduated from high school while behind barbed wire.

The meeting of the authors' minds culminated in an all day program given at UCLA which had for its theme, "Can it happen again?" The reference, of course, was to the wartime evacuation of the Japanese and both authors participated in the planning and giving of the major presentation.

We have different academic as well as different existential backgrounds. Kitano was trained as a social scientist, Daniels as a historian. We are attempting that oft-praised but rarely attempted endeavor, the inter-disciplinary approach. This work was jointly conceived and planned: although each author has different primary responsibilities, each section is a mutual production.

The result, we hope, will stimulate others to look at this terribly complex problem from new directions. Finding new answers is undeniably a question of some urgency, for if anything is clear about what may be an American dilemma, it is that the old, gradualist, accommodationist answers, however logical, just do not work. As Du Bois so clearly stated: "Either the United States will destroy ignorance or ignorance will destroy the United States."

We have had more valuable assistance from many hands than we can adequately acknowledge here. Special thanks are due to Robert Conhaim, then of UCLA Extension, who helped us plan our first collaborative effort, the symposium from which this book grew. Neil Smelser read an early draft and made cogent and provocative criticisms. Nathan Cohen, James Dimitroff, John Modell, and Douglas Nelson each made significant contributions. Judith Daniels listened to and helped shape much of the manuscript and proofread it all. Mrs. Helen Harris of Prentice-Hall edited with intelligence and dispatch. The Japanese-American Research Project and its administrator, Joe Grant Masaoka, were most generous in sharing resources. The faculty research committee at UCLA provided a travel grant and Miss Carol Hansen and Mrs. Diane Larsen typed most of the manuscript.

Finally, but not least in importance, we would like to express our appreciation to our students, graduate and undergraduate, with whom we have explored some of the dimensions of ethnicity in America. Their heartfelt intensity about minority problems and history has been a constant stimulus. Each of us has participated in a variety of civil rights and economic opportunity programs, both public and private. We have gained from our participation in these endeavors with members of ethnic communities and concerned representatives of the majority culture, much more than we have been able to contribute. Research and teaching, theory and practice, contemplation and action are not the dichotomies that so many superficial observers suppose; on the contrary, they represent linked aspects of meaningful, contemporary, academic experience. Whatever merits this book may have, flow, we think, from our participation in both sides of that experience.

ROGER DANIELS
HARRY H. L. KITANO

Contents

AMERICAN RACISM:

Exploration of the Nature of Prejudice

1

Racism:
The Whites and Non Whites

In March 1968, the National Advisory Commission on Civil Disorders appointed by the President reported its conclusions to the American people.[1] Its basic finding, more bromide than bombshell to those sophisticated in race relations, was simply:

> What white Americans have never fully understood—but what the Negro can never forget—is that white society is deeply implicated in the ghetto. White institutions created it, white institutions maintain it, and white society condones it.[2]

And again,

> Of the basic causes, the most fundamental is the racial attitude and behavior of white Americans toward black Americans. Race prejudice has shaped our history decisively: it now threatens to affect our future. White racism is essentially responsible for the explosive mixture that has been accumulating in our cities. . . .[3]

[1] The term nonwhites is a poor one. As Herman Blake, a black sociologist, said in a conversation, "If you're a male, would you like to be referred to as a nonfemale?"

[2] National Advisory Commission on Civil Disorders, *Report* (New York: Grosset & Dunlap, Inc., 1968), p. 2.

[3] *Ibid.*, p. 10.

1

Yet these largely self-evident conclusions, reached by a commission of moderate members of the Establishment, set off a reaction of disbelief and disclaimer. It was not surprising that conservatives on the race question, those who frequently use the phrase "law and order" to mask their prejudices, should reject these and other conclusions stated in the report. But many "liberals" rejected them as well. Perhaps the most illuminating of these reactions came from Max Ascoli, the European-born editor of the liberal periodical *The Reporter*. He found it "a pity, a very great pity" that the usefulness of the report was "impaired by the verbal recklessness of a few phrases," the chief of which was "white racism." This idea Ascoli vehemently rejected; racism was something he had left behind in Europe, something alien to America.

> Racism is an ideology forever tied to the memory of Hitler's Germany. It has an unredeemable quality which no one can shake off, and for which no exception can be made. We have had in this country, and to our shame we still have, a number of prejudices against Negroes—probably stronger against them because of their number and their inferior condition than against other minority groups. But prejudice, unlike racism, is not a belief.[4]

There is more to this denial than semantics; Ascoli's denial—and the less articulate denials of many liberals—are essentially denials of guilt, both for themselves and for the society for which they speak. And, at least inferentially, it is a suggestion that somehow the fault, or part of it, must lie with the blacks. The assessment of guilt, the attribution of fault, is not, however, the aim of this book. Its aim is first to define and then to illustrate how the phenomenon of "white racism" came about.

Racism, as used here, means very simply the belief that one or more races have innate superiority over other races. This must be distinguished from ethnocentrism, the belief that one's own group is the best or superior to all others. While the latter is a seemingly universal phenomenon, dating back to the dimmest frontiers of time, racism is a product of the modern world of the last three or four centuries.

There is no one basic definition of racism, but there is some

---

[4] Max Ascoli, "Of Black and White," *The Reporter*, March 21, 1968, p. 14.

agreement that, at least in part, one would include some of the following points:

1. There is little validity in the doctrine of racial equality; some races are demonstrably superior to others.
2. Races can be graded in terms of superiority. The Caucasian is presumed to be superior, and history is used to validate this claim. Caucasians have constantly shown their physical and mental superiority.
3. Nations and peoples who have interbred with the nonwhite races do not progress, and countries controlled by nonwhites do not progress.
4. Amalgamation means the wiping out of the superior Caucasian race, a process which leads to the eventual decline of a civilization.

What the riot commission called "white racism" is a product of the expansion of Europe, of the technological superiority which, from its beginning in the late fifteenth century, allowed Europeans to dominate the entire world. (For the purpose of this discussion, the United States, the British Dominions, and the Union of South Africa should be considered extensions of Europe.) The political domination by Europe, which began to assert itself with the Portuguese and Spanish conquests of the late fifteenth century, has come to an end. (The Indian historian, K. M. Pannikar, understanding this, has written of a Vasco da Gama epoch, dating from 1498 to 1945, as being the only period in Asian history in which that continent's destiny was controlled by non-Asians.[5]) Not surprisingly, Europeans came to associate their undeniable technological success with some kind of innate superiority, a belief that was substantiated by their established control over the non-European people. The Indians of Mexico, for example, associated the invincible conquistadores with the gods themselves. Slowly but surely, throughout the sixteenth and seventeenth centuries, the objective circumstances of history lent credence to the utterly mistaken notion that white men were superior to all others.

To see how new this idea was, one need only look at the most fascinating of all medieval adventure narratives, *The Travels of Marco Polo*. Polo, an Italian commercial traveler who visited China

[5] Kavalam M. Pannikar, *Asia and Western Dominance: A Survey of the Vasco da Gama Epoch of Asian History, 1498–1945* (New York: Humanities Press, Inc., 1959).

in the late thirteenth century, writes not from a point of view of superiority, but as a visitor from an underdeveloped nation appreciating a developed one. Some three centuries later, at the beginning of the English colonization of America, ideas of inherent superiority were so little developed that when John Rolfe made the first interracial marriage with Pocahontas in 1614, the couple was presented at the English court, something that would have been impossible a few decades later. By the end of the seventeenth century, the European assumption of superiority was fully established. Whatever national and parochial loyalties might divide Europeans at home, in the frontier areas which they were exploiting they began to view white men as a distinct class. This was true wherever Europeans came into contact with men of color: in Asia, in the Antipodes, in Africa, and in North and South America. If, in each of these areas, a somewhat different result ensued, it was due to the different technological, geographical, political, economic, and demographic circumstances. For example, when encountering the complex civilizations of Asia, the colonial powers merely imposed a numerically small superstructure upon the existing civilizations, allowing "good" native rulers to maintain a great deal of power. In the final analysis, an essentially Asian culture has remained, though with European overtones. But in the Antipodes and much of North America, the Europeans found a thin population of backward peoples, pushed them into less desirable areas, and in the process destroyed many of them. (In Tasmania and some islands of the West Indies, actual genocide occurred.) In Mexico and much of South America, a numerically small superstructure was imposed, as in Asia, but in the New World the resulting cultural mix was perhaps more European than Indian. In sub-Saharan Africa, where indigenous cultures were less developed than in Asia or the more advanced areas of the New World, an entirely different cultural mixture has emerged, a mixture that is probably closer to the Latin American than to the Asian model. A very long book could be written narrating the circumstances of these various racial conflicts. We have chosen, however, to concentrate on racism in America (that is, the United States of America) and to use the experience of one region, California, as our example.

Our reasons for this are varied. We do not mean to suggest that California is the worst example of American racism. Rather, it is one of the most interesting, partly because of the diverse nature of its history of ethnic conflict, partly because it has "solved" several of its ethnic problems, and partly because, until very recently, the bottom rung on the ladder of ethnic acceptability has been occupied by groups other than the Negro—a rare phenomenon in American history. Finally, as a frontier area—a frontier first of New Spain, then of Mexico, and finally of the United States (and, in other senses, a frontier of China and Japan, and of the urban and now megalopolitan frontiers)—it has reflected the ethnic mores of the parent societies while at the same time it set the style for new kinds of interracial conflict. In focusing on California, then, we really focus on the nation. We hope to do so through the prism of California's unique experience and thus perhaps see the whole from a new angle.

Major Perspective

The major assumption in our perspective on race relations rests on a two-category system.[6] By "two-category" we mean a system of stratification that is divided into two broad categories: the white and the nonwhite. We readily acknowledge that there are many other stratification systems (e.g., social class, age-generation) and that racial categories are not relevant in all circumstances. Further, a separate and discrete two-category system may never be found in a "pure" state, although the model of slavery surely approaches this "ideal." Generally, the two-category system refers to a paternalistic structure—that is, one group presumes superiority over the other, so that the following diagram is illustrative:

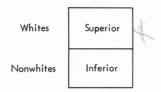

Figure 1. The two-category system of race relations. All whites are viewed as superior to all nonwhites.

The convenience of the stratification is one of its most important qualities. Physical visibility, based primarily on skin color, means that a quick differentiation and discrimination can be established.

---

[6] A term used by Lloyd Warner in *American Life: Dream and Reality* (Chicago: University of Chicago Press, 1953), pp. 17–19.

America has often used a two-category system for discriminative purposes. The two-party system; the "good guys" versus the "bad guys"; the hero versus the villain; the communist versus the noncommunist; and the "haves" versus the "have nots" are common examples of the use of binary models, to handle the problems both of man and of the computer. The categorization and subsequent labeling is important since such a process often permits actions against the "enemy" which are frowned upon in normal, everyday life. The most extreme behavior is likely to occur when the stratification encourages one group to view the other as less than human. Whites have often looked upon the relationship between themselves and nonwhites in these terms—nonwhites have heard themselves referred to as monkeys or dogs, or as breeding like rabbits. Other common comparisons include the owner-to-chattel and the adult-to-child relationships.

These techniques of "neutralization"[7] permit certain rationalizations or justifications for behavior ranging from restrictive and discriminatory laws to outright acts of violence. Conversely, actions are often stalled when other than a two-category system is conceived, since the grays and the in-betweens call for discriminative functions that can lead to confusion, hesitation, and inaction.

The major projected outcome of the two-category system is that every white man, no matter how "low," is above every nonwhite, no matter how "high." This dichotomy holds true on all levels—education, economics, politics, and the social-psychological spheres.

As Banton, the anthropologist, indicates, the problem of maintaining two categories means that:

> . . . a great variety of other institutions and patterns have to be organized to take account of, and support this distinction. There must be a strain towards consistency among the institutions of a society, or it will disintegrate.[8]

From this perspective, our first major area for analysis will deal with the structures and institutions which have been developed to

[7] The term is used by G. Sykes and D. Matza, "Techniques of Neutralization: A Theory of Delinquency," *American Sociological Review*, December 1957, 22: 664–70, in relation to criminal and delinquent behavior. In order to justify certain actions, the victim is "neutralized," that is, he is defined as "deserving what he got." It serves a function similar to the psychoanalytic concept of rationalization, again a justification for doing what is wrong.

[8] Michael Banton, *Race Relations* (London: Tavistock Publications, 1967), p. 115.

maintain the two-category system. We refer to "boundary maintenance," or to the set of beliefs, attitudes, organizations, structures,
institutions, and mechanisms which support the distinction between
races. The legal system, labor unions, employers, educational institutions, the mass media, voluntary organizations, and the like are
structures that have actively maintained feelings of superiority that
are symptomatic of or associated with white racism. Moreover, it is
important to realize that attitudes of superiority and the desire to
uphold the status quo structures are held by many "normal," decent,
and honorable men.

For example, a study by Kitano [9] emphasizes the role of the
"normal" personality and discrimination. Contrary to the common
explanation of linking personality disturbance and discriminatory
behavior, the research explained the phenomenon with a different
relationship. The normal person, strongly identified with his group,
will tend to limit social interaction with other groups. Conversely, the
"marginal" person will tend to cross structural lines. Therefore, the
normal person may be much more discriminatory toward other
groups than the marginal person.

The second major area for analysis will deal with those groups
located on the other side of the two-category system. They are the
nonwhites, the groups that feel the walls and boundaries and are
forced to adapt to their subservient status. The size of these
groups, their goals, their organization, their cohesion, and their
culture determine the type and quality of interaction between the
races.

The groups with cultures most congruent with American middle-
class mores (e.g., stress on education and hard work) will tend to
adapt with the least amount of overt, conflictive behavior. But in the
process of acculturation, these groups may lose their unique identities, so that the question of "success" eventually hinges upon an
emotional value question.

The final question for us to answer is, "Can it happen again?"
We are referring to such solutions to our racial problems as concentration camps, apartheid, and genocide. By presenting the circumstances behind the use of such extreme solutions, we obviously hope
that it will never happen again.

[9] Harry H. L. Kitano, "Passive Discrimination: The Normal Person," *The
Journal of Social Psychology*, 1966, **70**: 23–31.

2

The Maintenance of
the Two-Category System

Ordinary Solutions

There is a belief that animals are most aggressive and dangerous when they feel that their territory is under attack. In the animal world, use of violence in defense of what is perceived as being one's own is looked upon as legitimate. Common observations support the idea that man may use similar "reasoning." "Keep off my property" and "Don't you dare take that, it's mine" are human reactions that imply the use of forceful behavior, including, if necessary, the taking of another man's life.

Our perspective emphasizes the primary importance of the development and defense of the boundaries—the separation between whites and nonwhites—as the key factor in race relations. For within the parameters of the two-category model, the development of the boundaries—the built-up feeling of what is considered one's own territory, of what are considered one's rights and prerogatives as white men—can lead to a defensive position that results in extreme solutions. And the reasons for both defensive reactions and extreme solutions are symbolized by remarks such as, "They're taking my job," "They're moving next door to me," or, "Do you want your daughter to marry one?"—extremely effective sentences because they can be personalized.

9

We believe that in racial relations drastic measures such as geno-cide, apartheid, and concentration camps flow from an initial attempt to maintain separation. Therefore, there is a logical development to actions that were initially motivated by a desire to maintain the "superiority" of one group over the other and to maintain the boundaries between them.

What we are discussing pertains to the hypothesized relationships among a series of destructive phenomena—race prejudice, discrimina-tion, segregation, concentration camps, apartheid, and genocide. It is our observation that all these actions stem from similar sources, and that they may be related in terms of a sequential development so that even the most extreme solution, genocide, is a possible alter-native if other proper conditions are present. And all these steps are related to the importance of "boundary maintenance."

Many of our current perspectives of violent behavior do not take such a developmental point of view. For example, one popular ex-planation behind acts of extreme violence is the "madman" or villain theory. From this perspective, lynchings, concentration camps, and the like are the result of a conspiracy between evil or sick men—men with a pathological bent, men with gross deviations, men with moral deformities. These men are not normal, according to the definitions of the larger society, so that the comment, "Oh, if we only knew," pro-vides a ready, and perhaps questionable, rationalization for the "good" people, whether they were the Germans at Auschwitz or the Americans at Tule Lake in 1944.

We feel that the consistent attacks on various racial groups are impossible to explain solely from the "sick personality" approach, unless one is willing to assume the existence of an extremely large number of such people, past, present, and possibly in the future. Per-haps there are other explanations, more relevant for understanding the constant racial troubles in our society.

Relationships Between Disparate Events

Under certain conditions, even the most civilized countries experience "rare occurrences." The death ovens at Buchenwald [1] were the products of a highly advanced, scientific society—the war-

---

[1] Although we are concentrating on the California experience, the Jewish experience in Germany should be mentioned since it is the most dramatic case of genocide in modern history.

time relocation camps for Japanese Americans were instigated by the most technologically advanced and progressive culture the world has known. At first glance, there is apparently only a tenuous linkage between such events as the past treatment of Jews in Germany, the past treatment of Japanese in California, and the current treatment of Negroes. Each occurred under a different regime, was aimed at a different population, and was the product of widely disparate ideals.

But are these events really so discrete? Is there a sequence—a process beginning with a two-category system and its inherent prejudice, leading to discrimination, then progressing to more drastic behaviors which are perhaps extensions of a prior series of acts?

From our perspective, there may well be such a developmental sequence. Perhaps final solutions are only possible when other shaping events have previously taken place. We hypothesize that the basic stages are prejudice and institutionalized discrimination. Therefore, we emphasize that concentration camps, lynchings, apartheid, and genocide are possible in any culture no matter how modern and civilized, *if the momentum established by a prior series of hypothesized stages and conditions is fulfilled.* Granted they are a logical series, an obviously paranoid leadership is not necessary.

The Four Stages of Maintaining the Two-Category System

We hypothesize four basic stages of racial separation. Each step is predicated upon certain beliefs, which in turn are translated into action-effects, and supported by primary mechanisms. We emphasize that all of these strategies for maintaining the two-category system are built upon a *basically false premise—that all whites are superior to all nonwhites.* Therefore, from our perspective, a sick society is one which uses increasingly repressive mechanisms to maintain the initial faulty premise; conversely, healthy societies (in a racial sense) are those which use milder mechanisms to handle racial problems.

The first three stages are "ordinary" stages; that is, they do not appear to be unusual responses to the racial problems in American life. A minority group member is born into this situation, and, without any effort on his part, finds himself avoided, stereotyped, and

TABLE I

THE FOUR STAGES OF MAINTAINING THE
TWO-CATEGORY SYSTEM

	Stages	Belief	Action-effects	Primary mechanisms
	1	Prejudice	Avoidance	Stereotyping, informally patterned rules governing interaction
Ordinary solutions {	2	Discrimination	Deprivation	More formal rules, norms, agreements; laws
	3	Segregation	Insulation	If the out-group is perceived as stepping over the line, there may be lynchings and other warnings.
Extraordinary solutions	4	A. Apartheid, concentration camps	Isolation	A major trigger such as war is necessary; out-group perceived as a real threat or danger to the existence of the host culture. Ordinary mechanisms (e.g., Stages 1, 2 and 3) have failed.
		B. Expulsion, exile	Exclusion	
		C. Extermination	Genocide	

victimized by prejudice (Stage 1), deprived through discriminatory laws (Stage 2), and insulated through segregation (Stage 3). Members of the majority are caught in a reciprocal position.

Stage 4 offers three cognate solutions—apartheid, expulsion, and extermination. These steps are "extraordinary" stages in that the nonwhite member must either "do something" or be perceived as able to "do something." The triggering mechanism may be external to the group (e.g., wartime evacuation of the Japanese), or it may arise from within the group (e.g., the Watts riot of 1965). Generally, the more severe the perceived danger, the more drastic the solution.

Each of the stages is related to mechanisms which enforce boundary maintenance. The mechanisms follow a developmental pattern. The simplest include norms or rules of etiquette governing patterns of interaction—the nonwhite may be called, "Hey, boy" "Hey, you," and his response may be, "Yes, sir." Stereotypes provide other "rules" for interaction so that there are relationships among the mechanism, the belief (prejudice), and the effect (avoidance). Similarly, the severity of the stage is related to the severity of the mechanism.

Laws are the primary mechanisms for maintaining discrimination and segregation. If laws (including norms and agreements) are perceived as having been broken and the nonwhite group or individual is perceived as being "too uppity," direct retaliatory action may be taken. Lynchings, house burnings, floggings, and boycotts are boundary maintenance mechanisms which may serve as "warnings" to intransigent nonwhites.

Extraordinary solutions are reactions to perceived extraordinary situations—the majority group perceives a threat to its existence. The triggering mechanism related to apartheid, expulsion, and extermination may be couched in terms of a formal declaration of war, or it may arise from incidents related to other boundary maintenance stages. The incident may lie outside the control of a target group (e.g., the Japanese evacuation), or it may lie in the target group's reaction to its pariah status. If our developmental perspective has validity, we should find that all those groups who have undergone Stage 4 "solutions" have also passed through the three prior stages.

We will present each of these stages with their appropriate beliefs and actions, with their hypothesized effects, with their presumed interdependence, and with their implications for race relations. Our perspective includes both the discriminator and the discriminated against. The interaction between the groups helps to determine the strategies and consequences of boundary maintenance.

When we mention the discriminator, or the majority culture, we refer primarily to the white Anglo-Saxon Protestant (WASP). He is our "national type" as represented by the *Mayflower,* George Washington, Davy Crockett, and Abraham Lincoln. Our national heroes and ideals are defined in this image; as Gordon says, "the essential outline of America has the Anglo-Saxon, general protestant stamp. The prior existence of Anglo-Saxon institutional forms as the norm, the pervasiveness of the English language, and the numerical dominance of the Anglo-Saxon population made this outcome inevitable." [2]

The three stages which describe the ordinary state of race relations in our culture are shown in Table 1. The stages are labeled avoidance, deprivation, and insulation with associated beliefs, attitudes, and actions of prejudice, discrimination, and segregation. Informal mechanisms such as stereotyping, as well as more formal sanctions such as laws, are used to maintain racial separation.

The three stages are dynamically interrelated. The most damaging step is Stage 2, deprivation, since its effects are so widespread. For example, through deprivation and discrimination an ethnic group may be less well prepared and achieve less, thus leading to what Robert Merton, the sociologist, labels the "self-fulfilling prophecy." [3]

AVOIDANCE AND PREJUDICE

The relationship between avoidance and prejudice is a relatively simple one. Prejudice leads one to make prejudgments of others; on the basis of these judgments, one simply avoids people one doesn't want to know. In this sense, avoidance and prejudice are inherent in any intergroup (or even intragroup) situation, and both serve a functional purpose. But prejudice is a two-edged sword. On the one hand, it prevents chaos in human relationships since it provides a screening device for selection. On the other hand, prejudgments and preferences based on racial grounds preclude interaction with certain groups.

Prejudice is an attitude, often negative, which is directed toward persons and groups. Concepts often associated with prejudice include ignorance, stereotyping, and feelings of inferiority and superiority. The important factor in racial prejudice is that people in an ethnic group are consistently perceived as being in "that category" and their treatment largely depends upon the ratings for that group.

Gordon Allport, a psychologist who has done pioneering work on prejudice, defines the problem this way: "Ethnic prejudice is an antipathy based upon a faulty or inflexible generalization. It may

[2] Milton Gordon, *Assimilation in American Life* (New York: Oxford University Press, 1964).

[3] Robert K. Merton, *Social Theory and Social Structure* (Glencoe, Ill.: The Free Press, 1957), p. 421.

be felt or expressed. It may be directed toward a group as a whole, or toward an individual because he is a member of that group."[4]

Our definition of prejudice is simply a "prejudgment of others." We imply that it may be positive or negative and that, given more information, an unprejudiced person may change. Conversely, a highly prejudiced person may retain his bias, even when more information is available.

Shibutani[5] mentions some of the complicating features in analyzing prejudice. Prejudice is not unidimensional; it is more than a simple response of being for or against someone; hence a rank order of preference is a gross oversimplification of the problem. For example, in the United States Negroes may be regarded as "inferior," but Jews may not, so that prejudice toward the Negro may involve a different constellation of factors than anti-Semitism.

The most common mechanism for maintaining prejudice is stereotyping. Stereotypes appear to be unique to each ethnic group. Each group develops a distinct set of cultural characteristics; each shapes the behavior of its members and enters into the American historical schema differently in terms of size, geographical location, and situation. An interesting question for analysis is the nature and content of stereotypes. Are they perhaps structurally determined, so that the group occupying the bottom of the ladder is viewed similarly, regardless of its color, nationality, or ethnic group? Or do certain reputations remain with certain groups, no matter what their position in the stratification system?

It is our position that certain structural commonalities and consistencies remain, and that recurrent ways of evaluating ethnic categories apparently depend upon relative group position in the system of stratification.[6] Therefore, we would expect stereotypes of groups at the bottom of the stratification to be similar. The California experience provides rich data for this hypothesis, since various nonwhite groups have resided in the basement at different historical periods. For example, in one era Orientals may be stereotyped as oversexed, criminal, dirty, and tending to lower property values. Do

[4] Gordon W. Allport, *The Nature of Prejudice* (Cambridge, Mass.: Addison Wesley Publishing Co., 1954).

[5] Tamotsu Shibutani and Kian Kwan, *Ethnic Stratification* (New York: The Macmillan Company, 1965), p. 95.

[6] A hypothesis of Tamotsu Shibutani, *ibid.*, p. 95.

other groups inherit this mantle when Orientals no longer constitute a primary target group?

Another important but often ignored factor in prejudice is the reaction of the target group. Most discussions of prejudice take only the majority point of view—that of the actor—whereas we will present the reactions of the target group, which vary in terms of its place in the stratification schema and in terms of its culture. For example, at one point in history a popular definition of a good Indian was a dead one. Did the Indian hold a reciprocal position—that a good white man was a dead one? Or did he react to prejudice with other perceptions?

We propose that the reactions of the Indian, the Japanese, the Mexican, and the Negro were varied, and that the interactional process—majority group prejudice and ethnic group reaction, majority reaction to the minority reaction, etc.—indicates the dynamic nature of the problem in a manner that more closely approximates the nature of prejudice than do relatively static models.

The model will also be expanded to include prejudices among nonwhite groups. For example, if the Japanese are the primary targets for prejudice and stereotyping, how do other Oriental groups, Negroes, and Mexican Americans react? Do they rush to defend the Japanese, or do they also participate in the process? Finally, the model is complete when we include the "within-group reactions," that is, the difficult choice faced by target group individuals who may adapt to prejudice by turning on their own group or even on themselves.

Why Prejudice?

A search for some basic causes of prejudice invariably leads to points of view based on scientific discipline. Some theories of prejudice emphasize the historical aspect; they regard slavery and Reconstruction as important variables in explaining the current Negro problem. Some theories lean toward an economic exploitation approach, emphasizing the functional nature of prejudice in maintaining an exploited group either for its labor or for its resources. A case may be made for urbanization, for industrialization, for the effects of materialism, depersonalization, and the mass culture; another point of view in explaining prejudice emphasizes mobility in our society, either upward or downward.

Broader theories, based on Hobbesian perspectives, find the roots of prejudice in the unsavory nature of man himself. Some theories emphasize prejudice as one outcome of the frustration-aggression model; others emphasize inadequate socialization and the development of the authoritarian personality, while others stress the importance of stereotypes. Each perspective can probably be partially validated with empirical data. But no one theory can explain every aspect of prejudice.

HOW CAN WE COMBAT PREJUDICE?

Another way of looking at the question, "Why prejudice?" is to ask, "What do we know about ways of combating prejudice?" This more pragmatic approach may help us to understand some of the dynamics of prejudice.

An apparently simple answer to the question is, "By personal contact, that is, by people from one part of the stratification system meeting people from another." However, this seemingly simple answer is in reality a vast enterprise.[7] For example, there are quantitative aspects of contact—frequency, duration, variety, and the number of people involved. There is the status aspect of the contact—is the minority member viewed as superior, equal, or inferior? There are role aspects of contact—questions of cooperative or competitive roles and of superordinate or subordinate roles. Further, there is the social context—is it voluntary or involuntary, and how are the contacts perceived by the actors? There is the personality variable—are the people high or low on the prejudice scale to begin with? And when other relevant questions are asked—about age, socioeconomic level, and previous experiences—the simple formula of placing groups in contact with each other raises more questions than it answers.

Nevertheless, research evidence indicates that contact is one way of combating prejudice. Deutsch and Collins [8] in their study of interracial housing reported the positive effects of Negro-white contacts. Raab and Lipset [9] report: "People who actually work with Negroes, especially as equals, develop positive attitudes towards working with

---

[7] Gordon W. Allport, *op. cit.*, pp. 262–81.

[8] Monroe Deutsch and Mary E. Collins, *Inter-racial Housing: A Psychological Evaluation of a Social Experiment* (Minneapolis, Minn.: University of Minnesota Press, 1951).

[9] Earl Raab and Seymour Lipset, *Prejudice and Society* (The Anti-defamation League of B'nai B'rith, 1959), p. 22.

Negroes. People who actually are neighbors of Negroes develop attitudes favorable towards being neighbors of Negroes. . . ."

Personal contact as a means of lessening prejudice is apparently most effective when a common task is shared on terms of social and economic equality and when interests or tastes run across ethnic lines. Further, the situation should encourage cooperative rather than competitive behavior, and, as in most learning situations, the contacts should be reinforcing for the persons involved.

If we assume the validity of these findings, the prospects for effecting any major change in prejudice through personal contact appear dim. The two-category system, with its separation of the races, precludes much meaningful contact for most people. The sole contact between whites and nonwhites is often a patterned interaction between employer and employee.

Even under a different model of society, such as the one presented by Gordon, the problem of structural separation remains. Gordon [10] comments that subgroups in our society have their own networks of cliques, clubs, organizations, and institutions which tend to confine primary group contacts of members "within the ethnic enclave," while interethnic contacts take place in considerable part only at the secondary level of employment and in the political and civic processes. Each ethnic group contains the usual class divisions, and the behavior patterns of members of the same class are very similar regardless of their race, religion, or national origin. But they do not go their similar ways together; "separated by the invisible but powerful barriers of ancestral identification and belief, they carry out their intimate life in the separate compartments of ethnicity which make up the vertical dimensions of the American social structure." [11]

It is from this perspective that we emphasize that prejudice is built into the very structures of our society. The "we-they" phenomenon, the "in-group-out-group," the "our team-their team" are symbolic of societal structures that emphasize the desirability of one identification over the other. And the most powerful identification, the grossest differences, and the sharpest prejudices appear to be related to race and color. Terms such as "unassimilable aliens" and "exotic cultures" are among the gentler reminders of presumed un-

---

[10] Milton Gordon, *Assimilation in American Life* (New York: Oxford University Press, 1964). Gordon's model can be viewed as a finer series of distinctions from our two-category stratification.
[11] *Ibid.*

acceptability; metaphors such as "Oil and water don't mix" sharpen the incompatibility theme, and pejoratives such as "yellow dogs," "filthy pigs," "dirty swine," "black bastards," and "lazy greasers" reflect the depth of feeling against certain groups.

Our line of thought resembles what Banton [12] terms "structural opposition," an interpretation in which a man is a member of a group of a certain kind by virtue of his nonmembership in other groups of the same kind. A person belongs to a tribe or its segment, and membership is activated when there is opposition to this tribe. Therefore, a man sees himself as a member of a group only in opposition to other groups, and he sees a member of another group as a member of a social unity, however much that unit may be split into opposing segments.

Banton feels that it may be more convenient to generalize the main proposition along the following principle: social groups form because, in response to stimuli, people choose to associate with certain persons and to oppose others. In its negative form the principle is even briefer; without stimuli there are no groups. [13]

We view prejudice as a two-edged sword. At best it provides an initial means of responding to others; at worst it precludes interaction with certain groups. Racial prejudice is a negative force since prejudgment based on race, especially in terms of superior-inferior, provides a systematic distortion of human relationships.

We assume that racial prejudice is learned, and that it derives from multiple sources, including individual, interpersonal, and societal factors. As with most attitudes, prejudice cannot be developed and maintained in isolation; therefore, the reinforcements provided by the social structures are critical. Even the most highly prejudiced people may find difficulty in maintaining certain positions unless there is some reinforcement for their point of view. And, unfortunately, the ethnic and racial divisions in our society provide ample reinforcement for a racially prejudiced position. Nevertheless, we feel that prejudice per se is not the major problem in our society.

DISCRIMINATION: THE MAJOR PROBLEM

Since our definition of prejudice stresses that it is basically a prejudgment of others, attempts at eradication appear to be virtually

[12] Michael Banton, *op. cit.*, p. 236.
[13] *Ibid.*, p. 65.

impossible. For if we visualize the needs that prejudice fulfills—promoting group unity and group identification, providing simple, initial cues for reacting to others, serving as a scapegoat and helping to "explain" social problems—then a not-so-facetious remark might well be, "If we did not have prejudice, we would probably have to invent it."

Assuming the function and prevalence of prejudice, the basic question becomes, "What can we do about it?" From our perspective the answer might well be "Not very much," at least in the sense of eradication. Instead, the focus should be on limiting the attitude (prejudice) from spilling out into behavior (discrimination) and its effect (deprivation). As MacIver says, "Wherever the direct attack is feasible, that is, the attack on discrimination itself, it is more promising than the indirect attack, that is, the attack on prejudice itself. It is more effective to challenge conditions than to challenge attitudes and feelings." [14]

The main danger of prejudice is that it may be "acted out" so that the detrimental distinctions are translated into behavior. For example, the prejudiced person may begin to exclude racial groups from employment or housing, or he may limit opportunities in the political, educational, or recreational areas. Or the limitations may be in the area of civil rights, such as voting, or the ownership of land, or the discrimination may be connected to restrictions in friendship, dating, or marriage.

Stage 2, discrimination and deprivation, and Stage 3, segregation and insulation, are *the most damaging steps in race relations.* They are effective because they are the primary independent variables that affect movement in disadvantaged directions. Discrimination is the necessary condition—the base line from which extraordinary acts can be broached as "solutions" for race problems. It remains the single most effective means of maintaining the boundaries of the two-category system.

The primary support for discrimination is "the law." As such, "law" may take the form of folkways, unstated norms (e.g., "Negroes won't want to live here"), agreements, understandings, or formal laws. Once a discriminatory law is passed, the target group is faced with a major problem. Consensus is against him; power relationships, unequal to begin with, are even more unbalanced because now the

[14] Robert M. MacIver, *The More Perfect Union* (New York: The Macmillan Company, 1948), p. 64.

entire legal enforcement machinery is lined up against the minority group member. And if these forces are deemed insufficient, the "uppity nigger" who oversteps the boundaries may be faced with other "boundary maintenance mechanisms" such as lynchings, burnings, or floggings.

SELF-VALIDATING EFFECTS   The self-validating effects of discrimination are described by Banton:

> Discrimination depresses the standard of members of the lower group in respect of health, education, manners and morals; this then seems to justify discrimination. Once they have been built into the social order, social distance and mutual resentment between the groups will grow. . . ." [15]

The effects of the "circle of validation" are felt by members of both the majority and the minority groups. The target individual finds that he has less job opportunity and earns less; he attends disadvantaged or culturally deprived schools; he lives in less desirable areas; he shops at less attractive stores with higher prices; his style of life thus becomes different from the majority group member. And damage to personality—self-doubt, self-hate, impulsive and often superstitious behavior, a resignation to fate and to his lower status—is common among those discriminated against. The target individual begins to see himself and his culture as inferior—his family less than adequate—his race as something to be denied or disguised as soon as possible.

Majority group roles are also affected. The majority group member may feel a noblesse oblige, a paternalism, a responsibility to do something for the inferior. Smugness, feelings of superiority, omnipotence, arrogance, insensitivity, and guilt are common by-products. Feelings of frustration and hostility are also directed at inferiors who somehow do not appear grateful for the favors dispensed.

COSTS TO SOCIETY   The costs of discrimination are high for the society in general. Lower-class areas usually produce a high proportion of delinquents, criminals, and mentally ill. The number of people living on public welfare is large, and the waste of talent and manpower through unfulfilled lives is a cost that goes far beyond

[15] Michael Banton, *Race Relations* (London: Tavistock Publications, 1967), p. 150.

mere dollars and cents. Phrases such as "equality and justice for all" emphasize the inconsistency between a society's ideals and its actual standards so that the image of a great society undeniably suffers from discriminatory practices. But of more importance from our perspective are some of the other consequences of discrimination and disadvantage. The probable use of apartheid, expulsion, and extermination is encouraged when discrimination and segregation have been in existence over a relatively long period of time. For discrimination provides conditions which virtually guarantee nonwhite inferiority.

DISCRIMINATION AND PREJUDICE

Although our previous examples of the relationship between prejudice and discrimination infer a cause-effect pattern (e.g., race prejudice leads to discrimination), there can be discrimination without prejudice, and prejudice without discrimination. For example, a football coach may personally detest Negroes but he may also give them equal opportunity on the playing field. Therefore, prejudice may not necessarily lead to discrimination. It is from this perspective that we indicate that prejudice is not the major problem. People who are not racially prejudiced may discriminate, a fact which, in the final analysis, maintains and validates the unworthiness of a racial minority and effectively insulates them from participating in the larger society.

The point made above is significant, especially when past discrimination and segregation have effectively relegated a group to a second-class position. Judging a man's worth by some standard (usually WASP norms), or using "objective assessments," may be as damaging as basing a decision on prejudice. For example, university admission standards (discrimination not directly related to race) that restrict entrance to a select group (e.g., from certain high schools) maintain the practice of insulation. Such a policy, although defensible from one point of view, ignores the unequal starting positions and the handicaps faced by ethnic minorities. Therefore, it is little wonder that relatively few Negroes and Mexicans are admitted to major universities (even if they apply) and that, even if admitted, their chances for successful completion are low.

The following cycle is illustrative:

The racial minority group has few models of successful college graduates. →   Even if a member remains in high school, he receives an inferior education. → When he applies to a major university, his chances for acceptance are low. → If accepted, his chances for successful graduation are low. → The racial minority has few models of successful college graduates.

The power of discriminatory behavior lies in its effectiveness in validating and maintaining the "inferiority" of a group. Once discrimination is institutionalized, it pervades the entire system so that those with racial prejudices find validation for their biased prejudgments, while those without initial racial prejudice eventually adhere to what has been known in the past as the "earned reputation" theory. Although few social scientists today subscribe wholly to this point of view, the attitude is still common in the general population. Such phrases as "If they'd only shape up," or "If they'd only keep their property up," or "It's really their own fault that they remain where they are," are still common. A more subtle version of the theory in the academic world is the "I'm doing it (denying admission) for their own good so they won't be hurt later." When does change take place?

Strategies of combat must identify the camouflage of discriminatory practices. The opening up of $100,000 homes on a nondiscriminatory basis may be viewed as a mild example. Conversely, one may suggest a "domino theory"—the network of discrimination is such that a toppling of one barrier may have an effect on all barriers. A suggested opening may be in the area of education. Better education creates demands for occupations and incomes, a process which in turn creates pressure in housing. However, the breaking of the barrier at any single point is not a simple procedure. The "culture" of the minority group may hinder change as effectively as the nonreceptivity of the larger community.

SEGREGATION

Step 3 in our perspective is segregation, which has the effect of formally insulating a group. It is a form of isolation which places limits upon social relations, communication, and contact. Segregation can be viewed as institutionalized discrimination which is enforced legally or by common custom. Thus it is most often observed in housing and social interaction.

Housing remains the most visible and most relevant target for segregationists. Terms such as the ghetto, the black belt, the *barrios,* Little Tokyo, or Chinatown are visible descriptions of segregation. The other interactions controlled by housing are as important as mere segregation itself. As Allport mentions,[16] housing segregation controls the schools that children attend, the stores, the medical facilities, and the churches. Friends and neighbors tend to come from among the segregated group, and if the housing happens to be overcrowded and poor (as it usually is), segregation and slum conditions become synonymous. Styles of life associated with these conditions (e.g., high crime rate, etc.) may also arise.

Segregation increases the social visibility of the group as well as marking off its boundaries so that problems of conflict and social control arise. Ethnic riots often occur along the "boundary" or when one group begins to move in on the other. Social control problems within segregated areas are usually quite difficult—policemen, firemen, and other representatives of the larger community are looked upon as intruders and are treated with hostility. Disturbances within the segregated areas are usually easy to "seal off" so that conflict across boundary lines can be controlled.

VOLUNTARY OR FORCED? Segregation can be voluntary or forced. The fundamental difference, in terms of our model, is a simple one—voluntary segregation is not built upon Stage 2, discrimination. Therefore, the larger social structure is perceived as more open, and mobility is potentially available. Under forced conditions, however, there is a lack of choice. Historically, ethnic segregation has usually been characterized by two factors—that of a forced nature and that of relatively long duration.

Segregation and insulation are convenient for the majority. There is now a location, a place where "that element" lives; there is some guarantee that voluntary or accidental confrontation can be minimized. There is also the opportunity to retain and sharpen discriminatory practices. Schools and services in racially segregated areas can be controlled in many ways, ranging from sheer political power to appeals of equality. "Equal" budgets and "equal" services (which are never equal) mean less experienced teachers, overcrowded schools, and a generally inferior education. And the same kind of vicious circle we have described in terms of discrimination operates under segregation, with similar negative effects. For example, under segregation:

[16] *Ibid.,* G. Allport, p. 269.

The lower status racial group member seldom meets whites on equal grounds. → He is born, reared, and educated under ghetto conditions. → Education and job opportunities on the "outside" require a different kind of background and experience. → His background limits his opportunities. → He seldom meets whites on equal grounds.

Segregation can also be convenient for the minority group member. He may feel more comfortable among his own "kind"—food, services, language, and customs are more attuned to his needs. He may not have to interact with his "superiors"—he can make friends and enjoy life within the segregated, ethnic enclave. And if he tries to leave, the white society may "warn" him to behave appropriately by burning his home.

An example of segregation arising from discrimination is described by Berry [17] in his discussion of the the Chinese in California. Some of the Chinese reacted to discriminatory legislation by fighting back through the courts, while others returned to their homeland. Some Chinese moved away from the Pacific Coast, but eventually most of them migrated to the larger California cities and proceeded to segregate themselves from the larger society. They withdrew socially, politically, economically, physically and psychologically. Most turned towards occupations less competitive with the whites and they developed their own temples, structures and institutions.

If the basic two-category system worked "perfectly" it would undoubtedly be a smoothly functioning one—groups would know their respective roles, expectations could be controlled, and the chances of major conflict would be minimal. However, even if we assume that the basic premise is a sound one, such a system would have to remain insulated from social and technological change. The Negro may not be content to remain a janitor, the Japanese a gardener, the Mexican a stoop laborer, no matter how honorable these positions might be. Or the segregated groups may not be content either to socialize within their own groups or to live in segregated areas. They may want their share of the American Dream. And equally as important, some members of the white community may believe in the American Dream along with them.

In summary, we have concentrated upon ordinary solutions or

[17] Brewton Berry, *Race and Ethnic Relations* (Boston: Houghton Mifflin Company, 1958), p. 288.

strategies in dealing with American racial problems. By ordinary, we refer to common boundary maintenance practices within the system which do not appear to call for extraordinary appeals for support—for extraordinary use of force and power in enforcement. However, it is a pathetic commentary on American values that we label our treatment of racial problems by means of avoidance, deprivation, and insulation, as ordinary.

EXTRAORDINARY SOLUTIONS

Often, avoidance, deprivation, and insulation are not deemed sufficient to maintain a two-category system. More drastic solutions appear necessary, although it is apparent that "ordinary solutions" —Stages 1, 2, and 3—create some of the very conditions that may eventually "necessitate" extraordinary solutions. By extraordinary we refer to such solutions as apartheid, expulsion, exile, and genocide. The purpose of these acts is clear; the majority society wishes to "remove" the target group by placing it more formally outside of the culture. The effects are isolation, exile, or even extermination.

However, in order to treat racial minorities in the above manner, certain events must occur either in fact or in the imagination. Probably the most common occurrences are those involving minority group behavior in relation to norms; if "they" break the law, if "they" violate some of the existing patterns, then "they" can be dealt with through isolation (jail), exile (prison), or extermination (the death sentence).

Some major theories look upon the social conditions (Stages 1, 2, and 3) and the "means-ends" discrepancy as central to crime and delinquency. For example, Merton,[18] and Cloward and Ohlin,[19] are sociologists who hypothesize that the discrepancies among expectations, lack of legitimate opportunities for fulfilling expectations, subsequent anomie and alienation, are major explanations of delinquent and criminal behavior.

Their perspective appears reasonable as one answer for the relatively heavy concentration of racial minorities in jails and prisons. Racial minorities are exposed to and yearn for the same goals of

[18] Robert Merton, *Social Theory and Social Structure* (Glencoe, Ill.: The Free Press, 1957).

[19] Richard Cloward and Lloyd Ohlin, *Delinquency and Opportunity* (Glencoe, Ill.: The Free Press, 1960).

success as do all Americans. Yet their chances for achieving the success goals are less because of Stages 1, 2, and 3. Blocked from success along more traditional and legitimate lines, they may turn to illegitimate means of achieving success. Breaking the law will then provide a reason for the majority to use more severe methods of boundary maintenance.

Nonwhites especially may remain somewhat skeptical of the Constitution and of the powers of the legal and judicial protections in our culture. It is important for them to realize that *extraordinary solutions can most easily be advanced during periods when constitutional guarantees become secondary to other goals.* We are referring to wars or wartime conditions, when "winning the war" and "facing the enemy" take priority over other issues. The most direct retaliatory action occurs when there is a state of war against the nonwhite target group, such as that which involved the Indian. Concentration camps and genocide are not unusual under such conditions.

A more recent example would be the wartime evacuation of the West Coast Japanese, including those with United States citizenship, to concentration camps. Their internment, interestingly enough, was justified through a series of legal maneuvers which may still be used today during wartime emergencies. It is no wonder that impatient politicians often clamor for a declaration of war so that swift action can be taken against those whose views and actions differ from their own.

Apartheid, expulsion, exile, and genocide can be thought of as desperate steps which occur when normal boundary maintenance techniques have failed, and society is searching for more drastic solutions. Perceived danger is the most common mechanism for triggering extreme acts. The danger may be real or unreal—it makes little difference because the target group has been so effectively insulated that the public is often ready to believe anything. In essence, the message is a clear one. One group does not want the other group to occupy the same system and is therefore opting for a one-category racial model through the elimination of the other group.

There is a hypothesized developmental process within Stage 4. Apartheid and isolation provide efficient conditions for successful genocide and extermination. Once a group is placed into concentration camps, the fatal step of genocide is not an impossible one. For example, in our section on the treatment of the Japanese American we speculate on a series of conditions which could have led to mass extermination once the group was already in the camps. The important point is that in our hypothesized sequence, goals of extermination or internment may not have to be initially conceived. But as each step unfolds, the next step becomes a possibility so that extraordinary solutions become more possible with each development.

It should be noted that the General Assembly of the United Nations passed a resolution on December 11, 1946, affirming that genocide is a crime under international law. Genocide was defined as any of the following acts committed with the intent to destroy, in whole or part, a national, ethnic, racial, or religious group, such as:

a. killing members of the group;
b. causing serious bodily or mental harm to members of the group;
c. deliberately inflicting on the group conditions of life calculated to bring about its physical destruction in whole or part;
d. imposing measures intended to prevent births within the group; and,
e. forcibly transferring children of the group to another group.

The resolution was ratified by twenty nations in 1951, but the United States did not sign.

Although the race problem in America is a result of various forces —economic, political, social, and psychological—it is, in the final analysis, a moral problem based on *values* and played in the arena of conscience. For the majority group can and usually has found newer and better rationalizations to justify its actions, so that arguments against racist positions based on facts and logic appear as a never-ending process.

Our perspective has been derived from actual situations. Before we proceed, therefore, it might be well to take a historical look at what happened to both the whites and the nonwhites in California.

3

Racism in Practice:
1769-1942

California was settled initially from two directions: its immigrants came north from Mexico and west from the "states." Each group brought with it a common contempt for the native Indian, but a contempt shaped by the quite different values of Ibero- and Anglo-America. Each group subjugated and suppressed the Indian in the quite different ways suggested by its own culture and its own experience with white-Indian relations. Each group ran roughshod over the Indians; each group regarded them as sub-human; neither accorded them any real say about their own destiny, except perhaps, to give them a choice of how they wanted to die—in hopeless battle or in an even more hopeless existence. California racism, then, dates back to the eighteenth century, back to the earliest settlement by Europeans.

The Mission System: Pastoral Racism

In all of California, in the late eighteenth century when the Spanish-Mexican settlement began, there were fewer than 250,000 Indians. (The great anthropologist A. L. Kroeber thought there were only 133,000.) Although this is a minuscule number by modern

29

standards, it was a much denser aboriginal population than existed in most of the rest of North America. The California Indians, existing in a relatively benign environment, were not particularly warlike. Their martial characteristics were much less developed than those of the Indians of the plains or the eastern forests. They fished, hunted, and gathered acorns.

Starting in 1769, the advance guard of European civilization began to push northward from Mexico. These Spanish-Mexican intruders did not come in large numbers; by the end of the Mexican period in the 1840s there were fewer than 10,000 persons of European ancestry in the province.

Although Ibero-Indian relations in California were not unpunctuated by the murder and massacre that were the typical challenge and response between white man and redskin on the rest of the continent, the classic relationship was that of an allegedly benevolent despotism in which the Indians were forced into a quasi-feudal mold and taught the virtues of agricultural labor and Christian worship. While no one can doubt that the Franciscan Fathers, who became the self-appointed spiritual and temporal overlords of those Indians whom they could corral and domesticate, were actuated by conceptions of Christian charity and duty—as Father Juan Crespi put it "for the greater glory of God through the conversion of souls"—the whole Christian-heathen dichotomy behind which the priests viewed the inhabitants effectively prevented them from seeing the Indians as men with human rights.[1] Apart from their immortal souls they were children to be protected, trained, and punished. For those Indians who became attached to the missions, economic problems were solved: food, clothing, and shelter were relatively abundant, certainly more so than they had been before the Europeans came. Nineteenth-century writers liked to speak of the "white man's burden" involved in training these "new-caught, sullen peoples, half-devil and half-child," but recent authorities with an anthropological and psychological orientation have questioned the utility of these enforced values. Missionization established the Indian as an inferior adjunct to an essentially pastoral-agricultural economy; more important, perhaps, it aimed at eradicating almost every trace of Indian culture. Some authorities feel that, in the final analysis, it was this systematic destruction of

[1] As cited in John W. Caughey, *California*, 2d ed. (Englewood Cliffs, N.J.: Prentice-Hall, Inc., 1953), pp. 108–9.

the nonmaterial aspects of the California Indian's culture which left him most defenseless in what the nineteenth century liked to call the struggle for existence, a struggle which the overwhelming majority of California Indians lost.

But missionization, however destructive of the nonmaterial culture of the California Indians, did provide for the mission neophytes the means of existence, and for some, the hope of a better life to come. After the dissolution of the mission communities, in both the Mexican (1822–1847) and American periods, much of the little that had been allowed the Indians was taken away. In the Mexican period the missions were secularized and the Indians attached to the missions were transformed into pastoral and agricultural workers on the various rancheros; shortly after the American annexation following the Mexican War, the American system of reservations was instituted. In keeping with what was already standard American practice, the Indians were almost invariably relocated on land the white man did not want. In March 1851 one of the first Indian agents in California wrote Washington that he had just concluded a treaty with six Northern California tribes which gave the Indians "all the land they demanded since this land was not of a character to be useful to whites." Just a year later, however, a more astute agent, recognizing that the great influx of Americans from the "states" promised to occupy "every habitable foot of ground in California," started the first California reservation.[2]

The reservation system provided for only a tiny minority of California's dwindling Indian population. After two decades of American occupation, the number of Indians had fallen drastically to an estimated 21,000; only 3,000 of these were under government protection on reservations. E. E. Dale, one of the premier historians of the American Indian, had observed that, under the reservation policy "the aggressive and warlike received consideration because they were dangerous, while the peaceful and inoffensive were neglected and furnished scant protection against unscrupulous whites."[3] Most of the decline in the population of the California Indian can be laid at the door of "peaceful" attrition by European civilization and its attendant diseases. Apart from the few on the squalid reservations, most California Indians were poor, landless and nomadic,

[2] Edward Everett Dale, *The Indians of the Southwest* (Norman, Okla.: University of Oklahoma Press, 1949), pp. 31–37.
[3] *Ibid.*, p. 38.

wandering sometimes over a fairly broad expanse of territory, some-times over a very restricted area. The Indian had no civil rights under American law; he was prohibited from giving evidence against white men; if arrested for "vagrancy," he could be farmed out to the highest bidder for a period which the law limited to four months, but which in practice must often have been longer; even children were often kidnapped and put into a service that must have been close to slavery. But to these dehumanizing and gradually decimating condi-tions—by 1900 the state's Indian population was down to about 10,000—was added occasionally a period of "warfare," which, for the tribe or group involved, was sometimes, quite literally, genocide.

This near extermination of California's Indian population was a relatively slow undramatic process. Most California Indians were not slaughtered; they just died, quietly and obscurely. An occasional protest—like Helen Hunt Jackson's *A Century of Dishonor* (1881)—was voiced, but little was done, or is being done, to alleviate the distress of the survivors. We really know very little about California Indian life and practically nothing about individual Indians.

One California Indian is known, and his story, as written by Theodora Kroeber, will have to stand as proxy for an otherwise un-known people.[4] Whether Ishi, as he was called, was "representa-tive," is, of course, a question that cannot be answered. There is no doubt about the quality of his story; it is one of almost unsurpassed horror. By a historical "accident," he was perhaps the last "wild" Indian—that is to say Stone Age Indian—in our part of North Amer-ica, the sole survivor, by a few years, of a people who were actually exterminated by other human beings.

Ishi's people, the Yahi, were a tiny "tribelet" of perhaps 2,000 souls occupying a few dozen square miles of territory north of Sacramento. In the space of one bloody year—1864—when Ishi was a small boy, all but a few dozen of his people were hunted down and destroyed by organized and legally sanctioned parties of armed whites. The survivors of this bloody year, perhaps fifty in all, were further harassed and hunted and killed for the next few years. Then, the surviving handful, a remnant of a remnant, went into what Mrs. Kroeber calls "the long concealment," which lasted about four decades. When, on August 29, 1911, an exhausted, middle-aged male

---

[4] Theodora Kroeber, *Ishi* (Berkeley and Los Angeles, Calif.: University of California Press, 1965).

Yahi Indian was captured near Oroville, California, the "tribelet" was down to a lone survivor, Ishi. He lived four and a half more years in the friendly "custody" of anthropologists at the University of California. When he died, of natural causes, on March 25, 1916, a minor variety of *homo sapiens* ceased to exist; the Yahi had become, in the words of our pioneer ancestors, "good Indians."

The fate of the Yahi, symbolically at least, can stand for both the majority of California's Indians and as a polar example of the way Americans have treated nonwhite peoples. But thousands of Indians did survive; some merged into the general population; the vast majority of ethnically identifiable Indians continue to exist on the fringes of American life, technically within our society, but actually almost wholly apart from it. Those surviving, less dramatic casualties of what one writer has called the transit of civilization from the old world to the new, also represent a kind of extreme example of white-nonwhite relations in America; physical and legal separation— what we would call in another land by another name.

The Californios

As previously noted, the Spanish-Mexicans who settled California toward the end of the eighteenth century were never very numerous. These Californios established a pastoral and highly stratified society in which a few dozen families controlled the whole province; an 1849 survey indicated that 200 families controlled some 14 million acres. It was a static society which some later romanticizers have made to seem edenic; it was a society, which, even before the military conquest by the United States, was being penetrated economically and otherwise by the aggressive Yankee from the "states." The almost comic opera character of California's position in the Mexican War need not be considered here; the Californios had no chance to repel the Americans and most of them knew it. The treaty of Guadalupe Hidalgo, signed with Mexico on February 2, 1848, seemed to guaranteed the land titles of the wealthy Californios, but in practice most of their holdings were quickly reduced and in many cases obliterated by Yankee legislation, enterprise, sharp practice, and worse. Henry George, in his *Progress and Poverty* (1879), described California land legislation in these years as a "history of greed, of perjury, of corruption, of spoliation and high-handed robbery." [5]

The treaty with Mexico also guaranteed full rights of citizenship to all former Mexican subjects, but this was honored largely in the breach. In short, the Californio became, at best, a second-class citizen in his own land; at worst, he became a "greaser," a despised pariah, little better off, in many cases, than the Indian. In the mining districts of the state in the 1850s the Latin miner, be he native Californian or immigrant Mexican or Chilean, was considered fair game for all. In many of the mining districts all "foreign" (that is, Latin) miners were summarily ordered out; many Californios turned to crime, but then so did many Americans. Gold-rush California was a notoriously non-law-abiding region, ruled more by, as John Caughey puts it, "their majesty the mob," than by due process of law.[6] The Harvard philosopher, Josiah Royce, one of the first great historians of California, ironically described the fate of the Californios: [7]

> . . . we did not massacre them wholesale, as Turks might have massacred them: that treatment we reserved for the defenseless Digger Indians, whose villages certain among our miners used on occasion to regard as targets for rifle practice, or to destroy them wholesale with fire, outrage, and murder, as if they had been so many wasps' nests in our gardens at home. Nay, the foreign miners, being civilized men, generally received "fair trials" . . . whenever they were accused. It was, however, considered safe by an average lynching jury in those days to convict a "greaser" on very moderate evidence if none better could be had. One could see his guilt so plainly written, we know, in his ugly swarthy face, before the trial began. Therefore the life of a Spanish American in the mines in the early days, if frequently profitable, was apt to be a little disagreeable. It served him right, of course. He had no business, as an alien, to come to the land that God had given us. And if he was a native Californian, or "greaser," then so much the worse for him. He was so much the more our born foe; we hated his whole degenerate, thieving, landowning, lazy and discontented race. Some of them

[5] As cited by Andrew Rolle, *California, A History* (New York: Thomas Y. Crowell Company, 1963), p. 306.

[6] John W. Caughey, *Their Majesties the Mob* (Chicago: University of Chicago Press, 1960).

[7] Josiah Royce, *California* (Boston: Houghton Mifflin Company, 1886), pp. 363–64.

were now even bandits; most of them by this time were, with our help, more or less drunkards; and it was not our fault if they were not all rascals! So they deserved no better.

Unlike the Indian, the Californio was not exterminated; he was swamped by the flood of immigration which swept over California during the second half of the nineteenth century. In the twentieth century a second and larger wave of immigrants coming north from Mexico would again produce conflict between Latin and Anglo cultures. In the intervening decades a few upper-class Californio families—who usually insisted that they were Spanish rather than Mexican—remained as subsidiary members of the California elite; once their rancheros had largely passed into Yankee hands, there was a romanticization of California's Mexican past. "Historic" pageants were reenacted, often with a symbolic Californio descendant like the actor Leo Carillo playing a feature part. But these ersatz histrionics were utterly divorced from the realities of Spanish-speaking California, which continued to exist in a subordinate position. Only in the 1960s, as we shall see, would Mexican Americans begin to protest more than a century of mistreatment by the Anglo majority.

The Chinese

If the treatment of the Indians and the Californios provided the historic foundation for racism in California, it was the Chinese and the various reactions to their coming, which began to establish the unique patterns of west coast racism. The Indian and the Spanish American were given similar treatment elsewhere; the Chinese were the first of several waves of Asian immigrants which have made the California experience unique. The Chinese began to come at about the time of the Gold Rush of 1849. Like most of those who came to California, economic motives seem to have predominated; in fact, the early Chinese characters for California can also be translated "Golden Mountain."

The first Chinese in California were well received; the state's racism was not yet catholic enough to include all men of color. The Chinese were naturally objects of curiosity, but since they were willing to provide supplemetnary rather than competitive economic services, there was little or no objection to them. This was demonstrated in August 1850, when Chinese, on two occasions, participated in San Francisco civic ceremonies, their colorful costumes, according to a local chronicler, making "a fine and pleasing appearance." This reception can be better understood once the fantastic inflation which the Gold Rush produced in California is taken into account. In San Francisco, in 1850, common labor received a dollar an hour; a dollar a day was common pay back in the "states." A loaf of bread, priced at about a nickel elsewhere, cost fifty cents in the city by the bay. Laundry rates were astronomical: prices as high as $20 per dozen items have been reported. Some Californians actually sent their dirty clothes to Honolulu and Canton. This inflation was a result of the gold strikes and an extreme shortage of women; those women who were in the labor force worked at more glamorous occupations than domestic service. Many Chinese quickly began to fill this labor vacuum. Jobs that are generally regarded as women's work were among the earliest points of entry into the labor market for the Chinese, and later for the Japanese.

But most Chinese, like most other forty-niners, eventually made their way into the diggings, and it was in the lawless mining regions that anti-Chinese feeling first broke out. By 1852, anti-Chinese feeling was already well-developed; it showed that curious mixture of class and race antagonism that was to be one of its hallmarks. One writer reports the following resolution passed by a miners' meeting:

> Be it resolved: That it is the duty of the miners to take the matter into their own hands . . . to erect such barriers as shall be sufficient to check this Asiatic inundation. . . . That the Capitalists, ship-owners and merchants and others who are encouraging or engaged in the importation of these burlesques on humanity would crowd their ships with the long-tailed, horned and cloven-hoofed inhabitants of the infernal regions [if they could make a profit on it].
>
> Resolved: That no Asiatic or South Sea Islander be permitted to mine in this district either for himself or for others, and that these resolutions shall be a part and parcel of our mining laws.[8]

Despite such resolutions, the Chinese population of California continued to grow; in 1852 there were an estimated 25,000 Chinese in the state; a decade later there were more than 50,000. Almost all

---

[8] Resolution of Columbia mining district, Tuolumne County, May 8, 1852, as cited in Alexander McLeod, *Pigtails and Golddust* (Caldwell, Idaho: The Caxton Printers, Ltd., 1947), p. 326.

of these were adult males; among the Chinese migrants males outnumbered females by at least 15 to 1; among contemporary European immigrants the figure was about 2½ to 1. Throughout the fifties, sixties, and seventies, Chinese amounted to ten percent or more of the population. Despite virulent opposition, the economic opportunities for Chinese in California were so great that they continued to come for three decades. The opposition against them was more than verbal; first in the mining districts, and then in the cities, Chinese were the victims of robbery, physical abuse, and murder. These crimes were rarely punished; the laxity of law enforcement in gold-rush California was notorious. Whatever chance a Chinese might have had to obtain justice was made nugatory by a ruling that no Chinese could testify against a white man. An 1849 law had provided that "no Black, or Mulatto person, or Indian, shall be allowed to give evidence in favor of, or against a white man." Five years later, the Chief Justice of the California Supreme Court, himself a member of the anti-immigrant Know Nothing or American Party, ruled that Chinese were included within the scope of the prohibition because:

> The anomalous spectacle of a distinct people, living in our community, recognizing no laws of this State except through necessity, bringing with them their prejudices and national feuds, in which they indulge in open violation of the law; whose mendacity is proverbial; a race of people whom nature has marked as inferior, and who are incapable of progress or intellectual development beyond a certain point, as their history has shown; differing in language, opinion, color, and physical conformation; between whom and ourselves nature has placed an impassable difference, is now presented and for them is claimed, not only the right to swear away the life of a citizen, but the further privilege of participating with us in administering the affairs of our Government.[9]

The Chief Justice was perhaps the first Californian to speculate publicly upon the possibility of an Oriental inundation, a fantasy which would later grip the western imagination under the rubric of the "yellow peril":

> The same rule which would admit them to testify, would admit them to all the equal rights of citizenship, and we might soon see

[9] *People v. Hall,* 4 *Cal.* 399 (1854).

them at the polls, in the jury box, upon the bench, and in our legislative halls.

The practical effect of this ruling was to declare open season on Chinese; since they worked together in gangs in the mining districts and generally lived apart from other miners, they could be and were robbed with impunity. They were the favorite victims for many Californio and Mexican bandits, who were delighted both with the ease of the pickings and with finding a group even more despised than themselves. It is often alleged that certain bandits, including the legendary Joaquin Murietta who has been made into a sort of California Robin Hood, delighted in tying Chinese together by their pigtails, suspending them over a branch, and then holding target practice! It was under such circumstances that the phrase "a Chinaman's chance," meaning no chance at all, came into the language.

Also in the early fifties, California governors and legislatures began to complain bitterly about Chinese immigration, and to make futile attempts to stop it. By the late sixties it was clear that a broad state-wide consensus was opposed to the presence of Chinese and that it was political suicide for anyone to speak up for them. There were two groups within the state that favored Chinese immigration: employers who wanted cheap labor and certain Protestant ministers who not only spoke for the economic interests of their upper middle-class parishioners, but who also looked toward China as a mission field with millions of souls to be saved and feared that their conversion might be impeded by bad treatment meted out to Chinese locally. The presence of Chinese, it should also be noted, produced two important transformations within the white community. The color question almost automatically promoted all white men and tended to blur lines of ethnic demarcation more rapidly than they were blurred elsewhere in the United States. In San Francisco there was probably more acceptance of Jews and Catholics than in any other contemporary American metropolis. Also, Chinese competition, real and imagined, produced in San Francisco workingmen a stronger sense of solidarity than in the rest of the United States, and as a result the bay city became the most highly unionized city in the country.

The Chinese issue smoldered in California during the late fifties and sixties, and then, at the end of the latter decade, burst into flames. The Census of 1870, which probably underestimated their number, showed that a fourth of the state's 50,000 Chinese lived in San Francisco, which had become the undisputed center of anti-Chinese agitation. The situation had been exacerbated by the constant inflow of immigrants (some 15,000 had arrived in 1870–71), the continued expulsion of Chinese from the mining districts, and, perhaps most crucial, the completion of the Central Pacific Railroad which had employed about 10,000 Chinese laborers. The increase in Chinese population, combined with a severe economic depression, produced an explosive situation throughout the state. In the sleepy village of Los Angeles, for example, some twenty Chinese were killed by gunfire and hanging on October 24, 1871, in an outrage that must have involved, in one way or another, most of the adult male inhabitants. But it was in San Francisco, in 1870, that the anti-Chinese movement came to a head.

The Chinese throughout California lived in distinct communities; probably one-half of them were clustered into the twelve-block confines of San Francisco's Chinatown. After the end of the construction of the Central Pacific Railroad, the Chinese, who already dominated the laundry business and filled most of the positions for domestic servants and menials, obtained employment in various manufacturing enterprises. In the shoe industry, for example, Chinese shoemakers soon outnumbered whites by 4 to 1; in the process, wages fell from $25 to $9 per week. In the cigar industry their dominance was even more marked; 91 percent (1657 workers) of all those employed were Chinese. In the textile industry the figure was 64 percent. In addition, Chinese operated many small retail and service shops. The economic competition that Chinese offered to white workers in the sixties and seventies was quite real, and was more and more strongly resented as the economic depression of the seventies lengthened and worsened. By the mid-1870s the "sand-lot" anti-Chinese meetings of the unemployed had already become a regular occurrence. Although the economic hardship of the 1870s was nationwide and its causes manifold, the working people of California tended to place most of the blame for it on the most obvious visible factor—the Chinese workman and the men who employed him. It apparently occurred to no one in the young California trade union movement to try to include Chinese in their organizations, so that a color bar was established that still remains largely effective. During the summer of 1870 anti-Chinese mass meetings flourished in San Francisco and other northern California cities, featuring slogans like: [10]

"We want no Slaves or Aristocrats"

"The Coolie Labor System Leaves us no Alternative
—Starvation or Disgrace"

"Mark the Man who would Crush us
to the Level of the Mongolian Slave—
We All Vote"

"Women's Rights and No More Chinese Chambermaids"

These meetings were addressed by labor leaders and agitators, including the soon to become famous Henry George. They passed resolutions demanding an end to Chinese immigration and calling for a battery of discriminatory acts against Asian immigrants.

State and local government responded quickly to the voice of the people. The legislature passed a patently unconstitutional act requiring a $500 bond for each Asian immigrant (regulation of immigration is exclusively a federal concern) while the city of San Francisco passed a number of frankly harassing ordinances with the stated intent of "driving [the Chinese] to other states." These included ordinances putting special taxes on Chinese laundries, a "Cubic Air" ordinance enforced only in Chinatown, which jailed the tenants rather than the landlords of overcrowded slum dwellings (critics quickly pointed out that the city jail, where Chinese offenders against this law were lodged, provided much less than the statutory 500 cubic feet per prisoner) and a Queue Ordinance, which placed a tax on pigtails. All of these invidious acts were eventually declared unconstitutional, thus adding to popular frustration. By the mid-seventies the California anti-Chinese agitation was noisy enough to attract a Congressional investigating committee which visited San Francisco in 1876.

The Committee, although "stacked" with an anti-Chinese majority (two of the five members were Californians and honorary vice-presidents of the Anti-Coolie Union of San Francisco), adopted an interesting and revealing procedure. The Committee attached to itself representatives of both pro- and anti-Chinese forces in California; these groups, and not the Committee, called witnesses. Each

[10] Elmer C. Sandmeyer, *The Anti-Chinese Movement in California* (Urbana, Ill.: University of Illinois Press, 1939), p. 47.

group was given the right to cross-examine the witnesses of the other. Thus, as in a court of law, most witnesses were first conducted through their testimony by a friendly interrogator and then subjected to a hostile cross-examination. In all, 128 witnesses, not one a Chinese, appeared before the Committee; about a quarter of them were favorable to the Chinese.

The burden of the anti-Chinese case was crude and effective; opponents of the Chinese argued that they not only lowered wages and thus the standard of living, but also that they were "unassimilable" and that their "heathen" customs were disgusting and tended to debauch others. The defenders of the Chinese insisted that without Chinese labor the development of California could not continue. They also denied the special immorality of the Chinese and did some ethnic mud-slinging of their own. The pro-Chinese people usually coupled their defense of the Asians with attacks on the Irish, the largest immigrant group in the state. (In the 1870s the Irish outnumbered Chinese, 75,000 to 60,000.) "The prejudiced Irish," according to the chief lawyer for the Chinese, were the real danger to the state and its institutions. They were, he insisted, "The same class that burned the hospitals in New York [a reference to the anti-draft riots of 1863] . . . who filled the Molly Maguire societies in Pennsylvania . . . [and were] the rabid anti-coolies here." [11] But despite the stress of morality on both sides, it is reasonably clear that most of those involved in the Chinese issue had an economic stake in the matter.

The employers of labor on a large scale welcomed the Chinese worker as a cheaper, more dependable and sometimes even more productive toiler than his white competitor. Charles Crocker, one of California's "Big Four" and the man responsible for the introduction of large numbers of Chinese into railroad construction—Chinese were often called "Crocker's Pets"—testified that although he had been initially doubtful of the ability of the slight Orientals to do heavy construction work, "today if I had a big job of work to get through quick with . . . I should take Chinese labor." Crocker argued, not very convincingly, that the presence of Chinese workers actually elevated white labor.

[11] United States Congress, *Report of the Joint Special Committee to Investigate Chinese Immigration*, 44th Cong., 2d Sess., Report #689, Washington, D.C., 1877, p. 56.

> . . . if Chinese labor was driven out of this state . . . white
> laborers . . . would have to come down from the elevated
> classes of labor they are now engaged in and take the place of
> these Chinamen. . . .[12]

Not surprisingly, large-scale farmers and ranchers tended toward
the same view. William W. Hollister, a Santa Barbara rancher who
grazed 50,000 sheep on 75,000 acres, testified that [13]

> My experience in this state makes me put Chinamen entirely
> above others. . . . I think that the future wealth of this country
> will be due to the advent of cheap labor.

The noneconomic support for the Chinese came from certain religious groups, especially those engaged in missionary activity among
the Chinese: Congregationalists, Baptists, Methodists, and Presby-
terians were the most active. Some ministers also expressed the
economic biases of their parishioners. The Reverend Augustus W.
Loomis, a Presbyterian, argued that Chinese ought to be kept in
California because [14]

> As soon as the Chinese were driven . . . away the artisans,
> employees, and servants [would ask for higher wages].

Under cross-examination the Reverend Loomis revealed a strong
anti-Catholic bias rather typical of those Establishment forces which
were pro-Chinese. When asked whether Chinese or Roman Catholic
immigration was more dangerous to American institutions, he openly
stated his fear of the latter. Few clergymen were prominent in the
anti-Chinese ranks, but one, the Jesuit priest James C. Bouchard, was
notoriously so. An effective orator, Bouchard delighted his working-
class followers with a lecture entitled "Chinaman or White Man,
Which?" In rolling periods he proclaimed that

> The man or the woman who would dismiss a faithful, virtuous
> servant because the wages were so much higher, to receive into
> the family one of these immoral creatures, because he will work at
> a lower rate—that would expose the children to be contaminated
> and ruined by such a wretch, scarcely deserves the name of a
> human being. . . . [The Chinese] are an idolatrous, vicious,
> corrupt and pusillanimous race. . . . It is the white race we

[12] *Ibid.*, pp. 666–68.
[13] *Ibid.*, pp. 766–67, 787.
[14] *Ibid.*, p. 458.

want. . . . The only race that has ever proved itself capable of self-government or really progressive civilization.[15]

Ironically, the author of these uncatholic utterances was himself of an "inferior" race; although he kept it a secret from his auditors, Bouchard was an American Indian. He seems to have been the only Catholic priest who entered into the debate, although many must have sympathized with the strong anti-Chinese feelings of most of their largely working-class parishioners. And it was the economic issue, most commentators agreed, that was the crux of the matter. One anti-Chinese witness, a Los Angeles newspaperman, claimed:

> I never found a strong advocate of Chinese immigration who was not actuated by fanaticism or selfishness. . . . I have seen men . . . American born, who certainly would, if I may use a strong expression, employ devils from Hell if the devils would work for 25 cents less than a white man, even though the white man had gone through all the rebellion [i.e. the Civil War].[16]

In 1877—the year that was punctuated by labor violence, riot, and the use of state militia and federal troops throughout the country, and in which many conservatives thought that the Paris Commune was being reenacted in America—the anti-Chinese movement found its most stormy leader, Denis Kearney, a San Francisco teamster and himself a recent immigrant from Ireland. Kearney, a born orator, kept reiterating an almost classic refrain—"The Chinese must GO!"—and embellished his tirades with incendiary slogans like: "every workingman should get a musket"; for the despised capitalists he suggested "a little judicious hanging," and for San Francisco, where he and his "sandlotters" flourished, he sometimes suggested burning. Like most American demagogues, Kearney's bark was worse than his bite, but he was the spokesman for large groups— probably the majority—of the population who had legitimate grievances in the harsh depression decade of the 1870s.

The Workingmen's Party, which was an outgrowth of Kearneyism, had a lot more to it than the anti-Chinese rhetoric which was its most salient characteristic. Its program, essentially a prelude to the Populism of the 1890s, called for such basic (and eventually forth-coming) reforms as: the eight-hour day, direct election of United

[15] As cited in John B. McGloin, *Eloquent Indian* (Stanford, Calif.: Stanford University Press, 1949), pp. 179–80.
[16] Report #689, p. 1062.

States Senators, compulsory education, an improvement of the monetary system, an end to corruption in public service, regulation of banking and industry (especially railroad), and a more equitable system of taxation. These demands, none of which were effectively realized at the time, were overshadowed by the simplistic and more easily realized cry for an end to Chinese immigration. A series of frightening (to conservatives) electoral victories for the Workingmen, including enough seats to hold the balance of power at the 1879 California Constitutional Convention, caused both major parties, first on the state and then on the national level, to embrace the anti-Chinese cause.

Accordingly, in 1882, Congress overwhelmingly passed a Chinese Exclusion Act which prohibited Chinese immigration for ten years. The Act was renewed for another decade in 1892, and made "permanent" in 1902.

California's nativist forces had thus, for the first but not the last time, imposed their will on a largely unconcerned nation. The American labor movement gave its support, but it is clear that political expediency rather than principled opposition was responsible for a majority of the congressional votes. Within the state, the old demand that the "Chinese Must Go!" quickly lost most of its force. Within a few decades most Californians, faced with a new threat of "yellow inundation" were remembering the then diminishing Chinese with a trace of nostalgia that would have shocked both the Kearneyites and their hapless targets.

The anti-Chinese movement of the sixties and seventies must be counted "successful," for it not only achieved an immediate goal, Chinese exclusion, but helped to shape a restrictive pattern to which our immigration laws adhered for almost a century. Some historians have judged this democratic "antidemocratic" manifestation as an aberration in our popular heritage. Professor Charles A. Barker, for example, in his monumental biography of Henry George, tells us that his subject's "Californian attitude toward Chinese immigration" was an exception to his "Jeffersonian and Jacksonian principles." [17] This, we think, is a basic misunderstanding of the period, and of the relationship between popular feeling and race. Jefferson and Jackson shared and perpetuated the racist prejudices of their own times, and those who have followed in their tradition

[17] Charles A. Barker, *Henry George* (New York: Oxford University Press, 1955), p. ix.

have usually done the same. In ethnic, if not in economic matters, enlightenment has been more prevalent among the upper than among the lower classes. And it is not surprising that this is so. In late nineteenth-century California, anti-Chinese attitudes were part and parcel of the struggle for the rights of labor. One can be repelled by the racist views expressed by George and other spokesmen for the workers and still realize that within the context of the times such views could hardly be otherwise.

Since, with the close of the frontier, free and unlimited immigration became primarily a source of cheap industrial labor, some kind of immigration restriction became almost a foregone conclusion, if organized labor was to grow and prosper. Few today can approve the racist and discriminatory forms that it took, but considering the times it was only to be expected. Federal immigration restriction legislation, which first discriminated against Asians, soon was directed against Southern and Eastern Europeans—the "new" immigrants who began to dominate the national immigration statistics from the 1880s on. Had the frontier—whose disappearance is traditionally dated around 1890—been exhausted while the "old" immigration was still dominant, a more equitable restrictive law might have ensued. Immigration restriction was originally fostered by forces that are usually labelled progressive; by the 1920s, when it became law, it had attracted broad support from the most reactionary elements in our national life. Liberal historians—and most historians are now liberals—have been reluctant to come to grips with this essential paradox of American life: movements for economic democracy have usually been violently opposed to a thoroughgoing ethnic democracy. Nowhere can this strain of American racism be seen more clearly than in the anti-Chinese movement.

The Japanese

The immigration of Japanese and the anti-Japanese movement which it produced in the first three decades of the twentieth century followed, in many of its essentials, the Chinese and anti-Chinese precedents of the late nineteenth century. The largely irrational reaction to the Japanese can be understood only in the light of the phobias against "yellow men" which the long struggle against the Chinese immigrant had produced. Despite this more than surface similarity, there were significant differences between the Chinese and the Japanese; differences stemming both from the disparity between their homelands and from the economic and social role each group played in California. China, at this time, was a geographical entity rather than a nation, and accordingly, carried little weight in the world; Japan was a rising Pacific power, and, especially after her stunning victory over Russia in 1905, one which demanded and to a degree obtained respect for herself and her citizens. Chinese, in the nineteenth century at least, remained alien adjuncts to both the economy and society; an almost exclusively male population, they spent their time after work almost completely separated from the rest of the population. Japanese immigration, on the other hand, adhered much more closely to the patterns created by immigrants from Europe: a heavily male group soon began to bring wives over and to have children, thus, establishing "normal" families. These native-born children (Nisei or second generation as opposed to Issei or first generation) in turn, although they lived in segregated enclaves, attended public schools and in other ways participated in civic life much more fully than the Chinese ever had. This successful "Americanization," coupled with a very "American," protestant ethic-like striving for economic success, ironically produced an even more intense hostility from the majority population than had the Chinese.

Agitation against the Japanese began in the early 1890s when there were just a few thousand Japanese in the entire state; it began, as one would expect, among trade unionists for whom anti-Orientalism was both an article of faith and a source of strength and unity. The famous anti-Chinese demagogue, Denis Kearney, tried to make a comeback on the new issue simply by changing his watchword to "The Japanese Must GO!" but, in the 1890s, even in race-conscious California, there were not enough Japanese for many people to become excited about; the census takers in 1900 could find only 10,000 in the population of almost 1.5 million. In the next decade, the Japanese population of the state quadrupled; between 1900 and 1910, 900,000 persons were added to the population of California, and some 30,000 of these were Japanese. Yet, this relatively tiny group became the focus of a mass movement whose international implications were serious enough to involve the diplomatic intervention of the President of the United States.

The clearest early manifestation of the intensity of anti-Japanese feeling was a campaign initiated by the *San Francisco Chronicle*, one of the two major newspapers in the bay city, in early 1905. The front-page headlines tell the story better than any summary.

CRIME AND POVERTY GO HAND IN HAND WITH ASIATIC LABOR

HOW JAPANESE IMMIGRATION COMPANIES OVER-RIDE LAWS

BROWN MEN ARE MADE CITIZENS ILLEGALLY

JAPANESE A MENACE TO AMERICAN WOMEN

BROWN MEN AS AN EVIL IN PUBLIC SCHOOLS

ADULT JAPANESE CROWD OUT CHILDREN

THE YELLOW PERIL—HOW JAPANESE CROWD OUT THE WHITE RACE

BROWN PERIL ASSUMES NATIONAL PROPORTIONS

BROWN ARTISANS STEAL BRAINS OF WHITES

There were, the *Chronicle* insisted, at least 100,000 Japanese already here, and, it argued, "the Japanese invasion" had hardly started. Like the *Chronicle*, most exclusionists constantly insisted—and many historians and sociologists still unwittingly follow them—that there were literally "hordes" of Japanese either here or on the way. In fact, Japanese immigration was only a drop in the bucket. During the first twenty-five years of this century, the entire period of Japanese immigration before exclusion, newcomers from Japan were just about numerically equal to one month's total immigration nationally. Japanese, immigrants and native-born combined, have never comprised more than two and one-tenth percent (.021) of the population of California and one-tenth of one percent (.001) of the population of the continental United States. This shocking disparity between the number of Japanese actually here and the reaction against them is probably the best possible indicator of the extra-rational fears and hatreds involved. The *Chronicle*'s anti-Japanese campaign, which was soon picked up by other papers, fell upon fertile soil. That spring, San Francisco trade unionists formed the first specifically anti-Japanese organization, the Asiatic Exclusion League. Politicians of all parties joined and abetted the hue and cry by making anti-Japanese speeches. The California legislature, by the unanimous vote of both houses, memorialized Congress to halt Japanese immigration, and supported the demand with a bill of particulars whose initial point—"Japanese laborers, by reason of race habits, mode of living, disposition, and general characteristics, are undesirable"—is representative of the whole. Or, to put it another way as did an Exclusion League orator, "an eternal law of nature has decreed that the white cannot assimilate the blood of another without corrupting the very springs of civilization." This naked racism was accepted by a broad coalition which included conservative politicians, like those who made up most of the legislature, liberal intellectuals, like famed sociologist E. A. Ross, almost the entire trade union movement, patriotic and fraternal groups and, shocking as it may seem, most of California's radicals including the Socialists. Jack London probably spoke for most of his supposedly revolutionary brethren when he declared, "I am first of all a white man and only then a Socialist."

In the following year, perhaps abetted by the social disorganization stemming from the devastating earthquake and fire of April 18, 1906, which leveled much of the city, hooliganism and mob violence against Japanese persons and property flared. There were almost a dozen separate incidents involving not immigrants, but four visiting Japanese scientists observing the damage caused by the earthquake. By fall, 1906, there was an organized campaign against Japanese businesses, almost all of which were small, personal service concerns. One victim reported, in the somewhat stilted translation supplied by the Japanese consulate:

> I am proprietor of Sunset City Laundry. Soon after the earthquake the persecutions became intolerable. My drivers were cconstantly attacked on the highway, my place of business defiled by rotten eggs and fruit; windows were smashed several times. . . . The miscreants are generally young men, 17 or 18 years old. Whenever newspapers attack the Japanese these roughs renew their misdeeds with redoubled vigor.[18]

The police, obviously sympathetic to the rowdies, did practically nothing; when a Japanese did bring a case, it was almost always dismissed for what one immigrant styled "insufficiency of evidence." Happily, there were no fatalities in the San Francisco disorders.

While the harassment campaign was at its height, the San Fran-

---

[18] Documentation for much of the material in this section may be found in Roger Daniels, *The Politics of Prejudice* (Berkeley and Los Angeles, Calif.: University of California Press, 1962). (An Atheneum paperback is in print.)

cisco Board of Education ordered all Japanese pupils, native- and foreign-born, to join the Chinese pupils in the segregated Oriental school which already existed in Chinatown. Although only a very few students were involved—at the time of the order there was a grand total of 93 Japanese students distributed among 23 different public schools and 25 of them were native-born citizens—this segregation order became an international *cause célèbre*. President Theodore Roosevelt, after hearing protests from the Japanese Ambassador, had Elihu Root, his Secretary of State, look into the matter. Root found that treaties with Japan guaranteed Japanese citizens certain civil rights in America, and Root felt that attendance at school was one of these rights. He had a federal suit prepared against San Francisco to protect the alien students from segregation. For the native Americans in an age when "separate but equal" was the law of the land, the law could do nothing; however, something could be done for aliens protected by a treaty.

President Roosevelt, characteristically chafing under the law's delay, took executive action. He summoned the school board members to Washington and with a combination of threats, pleas, cajolings, and promises, succeeded in having the school board rescind the offending order. At about the same time—early 1907— he managed to prevent the California legislature from passing anti-Japanese legislation. In return for this restraint, which was highly unpopular among most Californians, the President promised to do something about Japanese immigration, which was after all the major concern. It was not so much the Japanese already in California, but the (largely imagined) threat of thousands more to come that was frightening. However unrealistic and irrational these fears, they were deeply and sincerely felt. While some politicians and others were able to make capital of the Japanese issue—as others had done with the Chinese—for most Californians there was little or no economic advantage to be gained from hostility to the immigrants.

Recognizing this hostility somewhat belatedly, the Roosevelt administration exchanged a series of notes with the Japanese government which have collectively become known as the "Gentleman's Agreement." Consummated in 1908, this series of notes committed the Japanese government itself to restrict the immigration of Japanese laborers and farmers to the United States. Both governments hoped this would quiet the agitation on the Pacific Coast and make it unnecessary for the United States to pass restrictive legislation barring Japanese, an affront which the prestige-conscious Asians wished to avoid. Had Roosevelt and Secretary of State Root understood the economic and demographic situation of the California Japanese, they might have pressed for a different kind of agreement. Japanese males outnumbered females in California by about 6 to 1. Under the Agreement it was perfectly correct for the Japanese government to issue passports for wives of Japanese residents in the United States. In many cases these wives had been selected for them in their native villages and the marriage ceremony completed by proxy, a procedure not only legal but traditional in Japan. In other instances, the prospective bridegroom made a quick trip to Japan and brought back a wife. These couples began to have babies; thus the Japanese population of California, despite the Gentleman's Agreement, continued to grow, a fact which infuriated the Californians, who were always ready to regard the government "back East" as enemy country.

In addition to this trans-Pacific migration, there was mobility within the state. As immigrant Japanese began to learn English and "the ropes," they moved out of the menial occupations that had characterized their entrance into the labor force and became farmers and proprietors of small businesses. By the end of World War I, Japanese farmers owned or leased almost half a million acres of agricultural land in California. This was about one percent of the land under cultivation in the state; on it the industrious immigrant farmers produced about ten percent of the dollar value of the state's crops. This outstanding performance was accomplished despite a great deal of harassment, legal and extra-legal. The major legal attack had come in 1913 when the progressive reform administration of Hiram Johnson passed an anti-alien land act which restricted the right to own land for agricultural purposes to those eligible to become citizens of the United States. Since the Japanese were presumed to be "aliens ineligible to citizenship" (the U.S. Supreme Court did not rule on the matter until 1922), Japanese were excluded although not specifically named. The 1913 act was not effective for three reasons. In the first place, many Japanese already owned land. In the second place, they could circumvent it legally by setting up local corporations or by leasing it. In the third place, they could put the land in the name of their children, who, if born in the United States, were citizens.

Hiram Johnson and his advisors had foreseen these evasions, but had pushed the law in order to increase their popularity within the state and on the national scene to embarrass their political rival, the democratic administration of Woodrow Wilson.

The seeming ineffectiveness of both types of control—the executive agreement to inhibit immigration and the state law to keep the Japanese from owning land—produced a great deal of frustration among Californians, frustration upon which politicians, demagogues, and agitators, sincere and insincere, played with great effect. During the tense years just after World War I—the years of the great red scare and of the even more pervasive fear of immigrants on both political and economic grounds—the anti-Japanese forces in California won their first great national victory, the total exclusion by national statute of further Japanese immigrants. Before that happened, the people of California demonstrated decisively their opposition to Japanese immigrants. In 1920 a massive petition campaign placed a stronger anti-Japanese land law on the state ballot. Under its terms (some of which were later ruled unconstitutional) all further transfers of land to Japanese nationals were prohibited as were all further leases of land to them. Similar bars were raised against any corporation in which Japanese held a majority of the stock.

A final provision, quickly struck down by the courts, barred noncitizen parents from serving as guardians for their minor children. The sovereign people of California approved this measure by an overwhelming 3 to 1 vote (668,483 to 222,086). Whatever else the anti-Japanese movement in California was, it was certainly popular. The 1920 measure, even had the courts not voided some of it, could not effectively change the role that Japanese played in agriculture, and most of the exclusionists knew it. Nothing short of expropriation could have removed most of them. In addition, the immigrant group had become so important in the production of fruits and vegetables, that a mass exodus would have created serious economic problems. These Japanese farmers, it should be understood, did not displace existing white farmers, but instead pioneered with new crops and new techniques in a market that was rapidly expanding (the state population more than doubled between 1900 and 1920). Unlike the Chinese, who directly competed with white labor, the Japanese in California took few jobs from whites and certainly did not lower wages. For most Californians, the major economic effect of the Japanese was largely cheaper fruits, vegetables, and flowers. There were probably a few thousand farmers economically disadvantaged by the Japanese, but this in no way explains the overwhelming sentiment against them; it can only be explained as a matter of race.

By the 1920s Americans in general and Californians in particular had been conditioned not only to an almost all pervasive doctrine of white supremacy, but also to the "fact" that the Japanese were the greatest single threat to their dominance. Otherwise intelligent and rational men wrote things about the Japanese that could be funny were they not so tragic. To cite merely one example, Valentine Stuart McClatchy, a major California newspaper publisher, a director of the Associated Press, and one of the most dedicated Japanophobes in the state apparently believed that:

> Careful tables of increase of the Japanese population in the United States . . . place the total in the United States . . . in 1923 at 318,000; in 1933 at 542,000; in 1943 at 875,000; in 1963 at 2,000,000; in 2003 at 10,000,000; and in 2063 at 100,000,000.

McClatchy compiled these "undisputable facts and figures" a few months before the 1920 Census found 111,010 Japanese, alien and citizen, in the entire country (71,952 in California). McClatchy believed, and persuaded many others to believe, that:

> The Japanese are less assimilable and more dangerous as residents in this country than any other of the peoples ineligible under our laws. . . . They come here specifically and professedly for the purpose of colonizing and establishing here permanently [their] race. They never cease being Japanese. . . . In pursuit of their intent to colonize this country with that race they seek to secure land and to found large families. . . . They have greater energy, greater determination, and greater ambition than the other yellow and brown races [and] the same low standards of living. . . . California regards herself as a frontier state. She has been making for 20 years the fight of the nation against [the] incoming of alien races whose peaceful penetration must in time with absolute certainty drive the white race to the wall. . . .

The views of McClatchy and men like him were standard delusions for the majority of Californians; the observer of the American scene in the 1960s is struck by the similarity in tone between McClatchy and the far right of today; both partake of what Richard Hofstadter calls the "paranoid style"; both manipulate imaginary statistics with seemingly devastating effect; and, perhaps most important, both see themselves as voices crying in the wilderness, voices trying desperately to warn a smug populace of impending doom. McClatchy, however, avoided a call for direct action; he was, after all, a high ranking member of the California establishment. Some in the movement were not so restrained. In Los Angeles, a "Swat the Jap" campaign developed, with a good deal of vandalism and hooliganism. In some agricultural communities, vigilantes ran Japanese out of town. At the lowest level, the sex argument was injected, despite the fact that miscegenation between Japanese and whites was almost nonexistent.

"Would you like your daughter to marry a Japanese?" asked the organ of the Native Sons of the Golden West, the most influential "civic" group in the state. "If not, demand . . . segregation of whites and Asiatics in the public schools." One leader of the group's women's auxiliary felt that California was being "Japanized" just as the South was being "Negroized," while still another woman described the Japanese mother as a "beast of burden." Similarly, United States Senator James D. Phelan, a San Francisco reformer, bewailed the fact that because of possible international complications, the Japanese could not be "treated as the negro." These views, and others like them, which we today tend to regard as extreme and "way out," were, in the 1920s, majority opinions featured in almost all the mass media. In newspapers, national magazines, books, and movies, the image of the treacherous "Jap" was relentlessly disseminated. In addition, the exclusionists had an action program whose major proposals were:

1. Continued barring of Asiatics from citizenship;
2. Rigorous exclusion of Japanese immigrants; and,
3. Amending the United States Constitution to bar even native-born Asians from citizenship.

The citizenship provision was settled definitely in 1922 by the United States Supreme Court in *Ozawa v. United States.* Ozawa, the individual filing the suit, was admittedly a superior applicant; he was a graduate of the University of California and of good character and reputation. The Court however, basing itself on the naturalization statutes which limited applicants for naturalization to "free white persons" and "persons of African descent," ruled against Ozawa, saying that the phrase "free white persons" meant Caucasians. Shortly thereafter, an applicant from India, who was ethnographically a Caucasian although his complexion was of a mahogany hue, applied for citizenship, citing *Ozawa* as precedent. He was turned down too; the Court (its personnel had not changed at all) now decided that "white" did not mean Caucasian at all, but meant, rather, "white" as commonly understood. If today we tend to think of the Supreme Court as perhaps the most effective voice of ethnic democracy, it should be remembered that just a few decades ago it was the last bulwark of racism, a bulwark that did not begin to crumble until justices appointed by Franklin Roosevelt came to dominate the court in the late 1930s and early 1940s.

The California exclusionists' second demand, exclusion, was won from Congress. Japanese actually enjoyed a special position under the immigration laws. Chinese had been barred in 1882; all other Asians, except Japanese, had been eliminated in 1917 by a "barred zone" provision in the immigration law of that year. (Japanese had been excepted because Japan was, at the time, an "ally" of the United States in the war against Germany.) It was also pointed out in Congress that the Gentleman's Agreement was effectively keeping out immigrant Japanese laborers.

In 1924 Congress was writing a totally new immigration law, one that not only discriminated against colored races but also discriminated against white ethnic groups—Catholics, Jews, and Greek Orthodox from Southern and Eastern Europe—who seemed undesirable and un-American to the WASP majority in Congress. If one were forced to choose a year in which racism and xenophobia seemed most triumphant, 1924 would be a good year to pick. In that year the admittedly prejudicial National Origins Quota System was enacted, and the second Ku Klux Klan, interested more in oppressing Catholics and Jews in the North and West than in keeping the seemingly quiescent southern Negro in his place, flourished. Americanism was being translated to mean not so much love of America as hatred of all things foreign, and quite symbolically, the quintessence of White-Anglo-Saxon-Protestantism, Calvin Coolidge, was elected President of the United States. All these things happened in a national climate of opinion that was blatantly racist. What seemed to be the verdant springtime of American racism—in retrospect it seems to have been its Indian summer—can be epitomized by best sellers of the time written by two eastern elitists of old American Protestant stock. Madison Grant and Lothrop

Stoddard provided in their several books an intellectual justification for American racism. (Similar arguments are still produced; the difference is that in the 1920s they were believed by the Establishment; today, such stuff is restricted to the rather sizable but lower-class group of people headed by George Wallace and his ilk.) Grant and Stoddard argued that

> the backbone of western civilization is racially Nordic, the Alpines and Mediterraneans being effective precisely to the extent to which they have been Nordicized and vitalized.

Grant, whose chief work was called *The Passing of the Great Race,* feared that if the great "Nordic race" should ultimately pass, "with it would pass what was called civilization." He saw the chief danger coming from Asia, which

> in the guise of Bolshevism with Semitic leadership and Chinese executioners, is organizing an assault upon Western Europe. . . .

But even more fearful was what Stoddard called *The Rising Tide of Color.*

> Colored migration is a universal peril, menacing every part of the white world. . . . The whole white race is exposed, immediately or ultimately, to the possibility of social sterilization and final replacement or absorption by the teeming colored races. . . . There is no immediate danger of the world being swamped by black blood. But there is a very immediate danger that the white stocks may be swamped by Asiatic blood. . . . Unless [the white] man erects and maintains artificial barriers [he will] *finally perish.*

In this atmosphere Congress performed a thorough overhaul of immigration legislation, an overhaul frankly racist but aimed at the anticipated flood of Europeans rather than at the trickle from Japan. (The official national statistics showed a net immigration of 3,200 in 1921; 2,000 in 1922; 2,800 in 1923, and in a last minute rush to get in before the ban took effect, 6,300 in 1924.) Almost all were women, brides or brides-to-be of Japanese men already resident in the U.S.; this predominantly female immigration after the Gentleman's Agreement cut the male-female ratio among the Japanese from almost 6 to 1 to about 6 to 4, and established the demographic basis for the Nisei and Sansei generations. The restriction plan upon which Congress finally settled was based on the seemingly equitable notion that national and ethnic quotas should stem from the numbers of persons of each nationality and ethnic group who had already come to America. If the 1920 census had been used, this would have provided sizable quotas for Eastern and Southern European nationalities. The restrictionist majority in Congress then decided, quite arbitrarily, to use the census of 1890—taken before the bulk of "objectionable" immigration had arrived. It was never contemplated that any Asian nation, other than Japan, be given a quota. The Japanese quota, based on the 1890 census would have been the minimum for any nation—a total of one hundred immigrants a year. But the west coast exclusionists, led by Senator Hiram Johnson, waged a sensational and successful fight to abrogate the Gentleman's Agreement by placing a bar on "aliens ineligible to citizenship," a bar that affected only one group of immigrants— the Japanese. This wanton act by Congress slipped one more dose of venom into the already poisoned cup of Japanese-American relations.

The third major goal of the California exclusionists—a constitutional amendment denying citizenship to the children of aliens ineligible to citizenship—was never close to becoming law; beyond the Pacific Coast there was practically no support for a measure which would have created a permanent caste of "aliens ineligible to citizenship," a disability which would have been handed down from father to son in perpetuity.

The native-born Japanese, then, were citizens, but they were no more full citizens of California than Negroes were full citizens of Mississippi. They did attend schools with whites, they did vote in elections, but in housing, the professions, social life, and even swimming pools, they found that, explicitly or covertly, there were "No Japs Allowed." Even when they won, they lost. When John Aiso, now a municipal court judge in Los Angeles, was declared the winner in an early round of an American Legion oratorical contest, a higher authority quickly decided that someone with a more acceptable skin, if inferior forensic ability, should be sent on to the finals in Washington, D.C. The second or Nisei generation grew up as legally citizens, but actually something less. Then, just as most of them were crossing the threshold between youth and adulthood, came indisputable proof of the inferior way in which they were regarded by their government: the Empire of Japan attacked the United States, and the United States, leader of the free world, spokesman for the oppressed and downtrodden throughout the world, put thousands of its citizens in concentration camps merely because some of their ancestors had been born in what was now an enemy land.

The evacuation of the West Coast Japanese—it is now generally agreed—was, in the words of Eugene V. Rostow, "our worst wartime mistake." Despite the contemporary claim that it was dictated by military necessity—a claim which the Supreme Court of the United States found valid—it is now clear that prejudice and politics mixed with fantasy, and not the realities of global warfare, were the controlling factors. In the months before Pearl Harbor, the rapidly maturing Nisei generation of native-born Japanese Americans were treated by the federal government at least, like other young men. After the peacetime draft was initiated in late 1940, Japanese-American youths were called along with everyone else, and they continued to serve after war came. The government had foreseen the war with Japan—naval officers had been talking and writing about Japan as "the most probable Pacific enemy" for almost half a century—and made reasonably modest plans to intern allegedly dangerous aliens. This was done by the Department of Justice in the days immediately following Pearl Harbor. It involved less than one percent of the more than 100,000 Japanese who lived in the continental United States.

In late December and early January, however, as the shocking war news from Pacific theaters grew worse and worse, a public demand began to grow for the government to "do something about the dangerous Japanese in our midst," particularly those in California. This demand was sparked by newspapers, the radio, politicians, and even some high officials of the federal government. The *Los Angeles Times,* a newspaper not particularly prejudiced against Japanese (by 1941 California standards), immediately reacted to Pearl Harbor by suggesting that local Japanese were dangerous. The paper editorially called for

> alert, keen-eyed civilians [who could be] of yeoman service in cooperating with the military and civilian authorities against spies, saboteurs and fifth columnists. We have thousands of Japanese here. . . . Some, perhaps many, are . . . good Americans. What the rest may be we do not know, nor can we take a chance in the light of yesterday's demonstrations that treachery and double-dealing are major Japanese weapons.

In the next weeks California papers were literally full of stories about Japanese espionage and sabotage within California; none of these things actually happened but they were believed. Some representative headlines (all from the December *Los Angeles Times*) would include:

JAP BOAT FLASHES MESSAGE ASHORE
ENEMY PLANES SIGHTED OVER CALIFORNIA COAST
TWO JAPANESE WITH MAPS AND ALIEN LITERATURE
  SEIZED
VEGETABLES FOUND FREE OF POISON
FOOD PLOT FEARS SPREAD
CHINESE ABLE TO SPOT JAP

Californians, soon to be followed by most Americans, quickly made a distinction between our enemies in World War II, a distinction dictated by racial prejudice rather than by the facts. A proper distinction was made between "good" and "bad" Germans—a welcome change from World War I—but few distinctions were made between Japanese. The evil deeds of Nazi Germany were the acts of bad men; the evil deeds of Tojo's Japan were the acts of a bad race. Had public officials and leaders provided some positive leadership, the racist Japanophobia might have been lessened or even stemmed, but instead most added fagots to the fire. The Governor of California, Cuthbert L. Olson, a liberal Democrat, had insisted before Pearl Harbor that Japanese Americans should enjoy all their rights and privileges even if war with Japan came. He correctly pointed out that equal protection under the law was a "basic tenet" of American government. But Olson's constitutional scruples were a casualty of Pearl Harbor; on December 8th, the Governor told the press that he was thinking of ordering all Japanese, aliens and citizens, to observe house arrest, in order "to avoid riot and disturbance."

On the federal level, the Department of Justice, although restrained in its round-up of some alien Japanese, did act much more harshly in terms of numbers interned, toward Japanese nationals than toward German nationals. It should also be noted, however, that more than a few young Nisei leaders applauded this early round-up and contrasted their own native son loyalty to the presumed disloyalty of many of the leaders of the Issei or immigrant generation. Other national leaders discriminated in other ways; even Fiorello La Guardia, who was for a time director of the federal Office of Civilian Defense as well as Mayor of New York, pointedly omitted mention of the Japanese in two public statements suggesting presumptive loyalty for German and Italian residents, alien or citizen. Seventeen years earlier La Guardia had been one of three congressmen to speak openly in favor of a Japanese quota, but in December 1941, he could find nothing good to say about Japanese.

But most damaging were the statements and actions that came from the military services and the politicians who ran them. The civilian head of the Navy, Frank Knox, returned from an inspection of Pearl Harbor in mid-December. In a statement that made front pages all across the country, Secretary Knox spoke of "treachery" at Pearl Harbor and insisted that much of the disaster there was caused by "the most effective fifth column work that's come out of this war, except in Norway." Our defeat at Pearl Harbor, as is now generally acknowledged, was caused largely by the unpreparedness and incompetence of the local military commanders, as Knox already knew. But rather than admit publicly that the Navy (and by extension its civilian chief) had been asleep at the switch, Knox, a newspaper publisher by profession, made the Japanese population of Hawaii the scapegoat to absolve naval blunderings. This big lie was reiterated a month later, when the hasty investigation of Pearl Harbor, headed by Supreme Court Justice Owen J. Roberts, culminated in a report to the public which stressed widespread espionage by Japanese residents in the islands as a major factor in the debacle.

But in the final analysis, it was the United States Army which was most responsible for the relocation. Within the Army, the loudest public voice calling for incarceration of the West Coast Japanese was Lieutenant General John L. De Witt, Commander of the Western Defense Command (the Pacific Coast). De Witt, who insisted that a "Jap was a Jap" whether alien or native-born, seems to have been inspired both by west coast civilian leaders and by many within the army bureaucracy. Eventually approval was granted by the civilian head of the Army, War Secretary Henry L. Stimson. Stimson and the War Department were opposed by Attorney General Francis Biddle and the Department of Justice. To settle this cabinet-level conflict, Stimson and his assistant, John J. McCloy, put it up to President Franklin D. Roosevelt on Wednesday afternoon, February 11, 1942. This was the real "day of infamy" as far as the constitution was concerned. They presented to the Commander-in-Chief a brief memorandum which listed four alternatives:

1. Is the President willing to authorize us to move Japanese citizens (i.e. citizens of the United States) as well as aliens from restricted areas?

2. Should we undertake withdrawal from the entire strip De Witt originally recommended, which involves a number of over 100,000 people, if we included both aliens and Japanese citizens?

3. Should we undertake the intermediate step involving, say 70,000, which includes large communities such as Los Angeles, San Diego and Seattle?

4. Should we take any lesser step such as the establishment of restricted areas around airplane plants and critical installations, even though General De Witt states that in several, at least, of the large communities this would be wasteful, involve difficult administration problems, and might be a source of more continuous irritation and trouble than 100 percent withdrawal from the area?

President Roosevelt ostensibly refused to choose; in a short telephone conversation he passed the decision-making power to two men who had never been elected to any office. The President surely knew what the consequences of his action would be. McCloy in turn telephoned a subordinate on the West Coast: "We have carte blanche to do what we want as far as the President is concerned." According to the Assistant Secretary, FDR's only qualification had been: "Be as reasonable as you can." [19] Although many factors must have entered into Roosevelt's mind as he acquiesced to the spokesmen for the military—the bad news from the war fronts, the pressures from west coast congressmen and their allies, and the fact that failure to do anything about the "menace" of the West Coast Japanese would provide ammunition for his political enemies —it seems clear enough that the President, too, held racist convictions about the Japanese, and that the notion that "once a Jap always a Jap" was not foreign to his thinking.

[19] For details see Stetson Conn, "The Decision to Evacuate the Japanese from the Pacific Coast (1942)," pp. 88–109 in Kent Roberts Greenfield, ed., *Command Decisions* (New York: Harcourt, Brace & World, Inc., 1959).

If it seems harsh thus to judge and label the greatest President of the twentieth century, it should be pointed out that racism is, unfortunately, an absolute term. It may be used to describe the most blatant demagogue and the most mildly prejudiced white liberal. FDR and his America were, during World War II, involved in an ironically ambiguous situation. On the one hand the United States was at war with the most viciously racist government of all time —Nazi Germany—and was committed to the destruction of that government and all it represented; on the other hand the United States was itself an officially racist country with a tradition of discrimination more than three centuries old. During the war itself we not only committed a new racist atrocity against the West Coast Japanese, but we also continued our long established oppression of Negroes and other dark-skinned citizens. We fought a war whose declared objectives were the Four Freedoms—freedom of speech and expression, freedom of worship, freedom from want, and freedom from fear—but, we did so with segregated armed forces on the fighting fronts and decidedly separate and unequal treatment at home. It was precisely this kind of dichotomy between stated ideals and actual practice that Gunnar Myrdal labeled the "American Dilemma." Franklin Roosevelt, like all Americans but even more than most, was caught on the horns of that dilemma. If he accepted the basic tenets of American practice, and in the case of the West Coast Japanese made it worse, he also shared in and advanced somewhat the American dream of equality. Some Japanese Americans were eventually allowed to enlist in all Nisei (white officered) combat units—the 100th Battalion and 442nd Regimental Combat Team— and the heroic performances of these units were certainly a causal component of the remarkable changes in the climate of opinion toward Japanese Americans that have taken place since 1942. FDR also, it must be noted, took a cautious first step toward real economic equality with the establishment of the federal Fair Employment Practices Committee in 1941. It is perhaps instructive to observe that both the FEPC and the establishment of concentration camps for the Japanese were effected by the same kind of legal instrument —a Presidential executive order. And both of these executive orders were forthcoming at least in part because special interest groups put pressure on the President—concerned white west coast citizens, local officials, congressmen, and the Army, in the latter instance, and Negro leader A. Philip Randolph's threatened "March on Washington," in the former. Roosevelt could thus be pushed into mitigating racism, but he could also be pushed into exacerbating it.

Once the President gave the green light, the forcible uprooting of more than 110,000 innocent people began. All Japanese in the three west coast states—alien and citizen, old and young, rich and poor—were evacuated to ten "relocation centers," barrack type communities surrounded by barbed wire and armed guards, located in inaccessible and largely barren areas in the interior of the United States from California to Arkansas. Even in this racist evacuation, the ambiguous character of American racism may be observed. The relatively small Japanese community in the rest of the United States was not disturbed, probably because it was not large enough to bother about and because no one was pressing for its removal. West Coast Japanese attending midwestern or eastern colleges and universities were not required to report to camp, and western Japanese already in the armed services were left there. Even more incongruous was the Hawaiian situation; Japanese there, except for the relative handful of "dangerous" enemy aliens, were allowed to remain at liberty and to go about their business. If the comparatively small number of West Coast Japanese was dangerous to the war effort, why were the Japanese of Hawaii—who represented about a third of the island's population—allowed to remain at liberty? The reasons were more practical than ideological: in the first place incarceration of a third of the population would have created serious labor shortages in what was to become the major base for the Pacific War and, in the second place, the mere logistics of removing more than 100,000 people to the mainland at a time when shipping space was at a premium, were insuperable. (One naval officer did however suggest that putting them all on the tiny island of Molokai, a leper colony, might do the trick.)

We will not describe here the trauma of the evacuation or the routine of camp life. (Kitano has done so in *Japanese Americans: The Evolution of a Subculture*, Prentice-Hall, Inc., 1969). Beyond the West Coast the internment received very little notice and most Americans east of the Rockies were probably only vaguely aware of it. The Japanese went quietly and voluntarily, as their leaders counselled. Schedules were published and posted, and they went in, in the same law-abiding manner in which they had lived their lives to that point. But were they law-abiding? Was the evacuation, necessary or not, legal? Stimson and McCloy for the War Department,

both lawyers, had been satisfied that it was "pretty much legal."
Neither Democratic California Governor Cuthbert L. Olson nor his
Republican Attorney General, Earl Warren, expressed any doubts
at all. The President signed the executive orders and Congress provided ex-post facto sanction. But what would the Supreme Court
say? In the months after the relocation the Court had three separate
chances to strike down the legality of the evacuation but, instead,
the justices merely struck out as far as civil liberties were concerned.

The first case, *Hirabayashi*, involved curfew violation. Gordon
Hirabayashi, a native son as were all the litigants (alien Japanese
were enemy aliens and had no rights at all), was arrested and convicted for refusing to obey a pre-evacuation curfew order by General De Witt. In a decision handed down on June 21, 1943—the war
was still in doubt—the Court upheld the General rather than the
citizen. Chief Justice Harlan Fiske Stone, speaking for a nondis-
senting but uneasy court, argued that:

> We cannot close our eyes to the fact demonstrated by experience,
> that in time of war residents having ethnic affiliations with an
> invading enemy may be a greater source of danger than those
> of a different ancestry.

The second and third cases—*Korematsu* and *Endo*—were handed
down during Christmas week of 1944, when final victory in the war
seemed assured. Fred Korematsu had simply failed to report at the
time and place prescribed for Japanese Americans in his part of
California. His attorneys argued that since the order was a violation
of constitutional guarantees, it was null and void. The Court simply
refused to judge. Justice Hugo Black, writing for the majority, insisted that:

> Korematsu was not excluded from [California] because of hos-
> tility to him or his race. He was excluded because we are at war
> with the Japanese Empire, because the properly constituted
> authorities feared an invasion of our West Coast and felt con-
> strained to take proper security measures, because they decided
> that the military urgency of the situation demanded that all
> citizens of Japanese ancestry be segregated from the West Coast
> and finally, because Congress, reposing its confidence in this time
> of war in our military leaders—as inevitably it must—determined
> that they should have the power to do just this. There was

evidence of disloyalty on the part of some, the military authorities considered that the need for action was great, and time was short. We cannot—by availing ourselves of the calm perspective of hindsight—now say that these actions were unjustified.

In a pithier concurrence, Justice William O. Douglas simply said: "We cannot sit in judgment on the military requirements of that hour."

Three justices, however, did so sit and found the judgment bad. Owen J. Roberts, Frank Murphy, and Robert L. Jackson all dissented sharply with their colleagues. Justice Murphy, we think, was most correct when he characterized Black's majority decision simply and bluntly as "a legalization of racism."

The third case involved Mitsuye Endo, a twenty-two-year-old native daughter of undisputed loyalty whose brother was serving in the Armed Forces. She went off to camp at the appointed time as ordered, but on July 13, 1942, her attorneys filed for a writ of habeas corpus, which, if granted, would secure her release. Two years and four months later—she was still in camp—the Court ordered her release but refused to inquire into the constitutional question of how she got there, much to the disgust of Justices Murphy and Roberts.

The Court thus made obeisance to the doctrine of "military necessity," in itself a dubious extra-legal criterion. But there was no "military necessity." As we now know, our top military planners did not fear an invasion of the West Coast in 1942 (some did fear an invasion of Hawaii). But, as we have seen, the Hawaiian Japanese went largely unmolested, while the West Coast Japanese were evacuated in toto. Without the crutch of military necessity—at best a weak one—the shaky legal underpinnings of the evacuation collapse completely, and we are left with Justice Murphy's bitter analysis—racism legalized.

But, legal or illegal, whatever the reasons, the forcible uprooting of more than 110,000 people who eventually wound up in ten God-forsaken camps in the name of a fictitious military necessity, was much more than an injustice to those involved. It has been argued that the evacuation was a good thing because it prevented the mass violence against Japanese Americans that many feel surely would have come. (Without attempting to justify the evacuation, Kitano, *Japanese Americans*, does point out some of the positive effects of the evacuation on some members of the community.) It seems to us, however, that in the final analysis, the significance of the evacuation goes far beyond any damage done to evacuees. The camps, after all, were reasonably humane; measured against the total human cost of World War II the damage done to the Japanese Americans was slight indeed. When, however, the national government, for whatever reason, is able to use prejudice to distort due process—and receive sanction for it from the Supreme Court—damage is done to the whole of society. As the late Morton Grodzins put it, the evacuation gave "precedent and constitutional authority for a policy of mass incarceration under military auspices. . . . That . . . betrayed all Americans." [20] The responsibility for that betrayal can, of course, be laid at the door of Franklin Roosevelt, and beyond him, with any number of political leaders and opinion molders, almost all of whom applauded the setting up of concentration camps for Americans on American soil. But more than individual guilt is involved; in true perspective, the relocation can be seen as "merely" one more poisoned draught from the bitter cup of American racism.

Just a year after Grodzins published the words quoted above, the Congress of the United States passed the "Emergency Detention Act of 1950." (It is a component part of the McCarran Act.) This law, still on the books, gives to civilians—the Attorney General is specifically named—the power that the military exercised during World War II, the power to put American citizens in concentration camps without trial. The purpose of the act is: "The detention of persons who there is reasonable grounds to believe will commit or conspire to commit espionage or sabotage. . . ." All it takes to put the process into motion is a presidential proclamation (an executive order) of an "Internal Security Emergency," which may be created, according to the statute, by

1. Invasion;
2. Declaration of War; and,
3. Insurrection within the United States.

Such camps were actually constructed and put into readiness during the early 1950s and apparently are now in mothballs. Quite obviously the precedents established in evacuating and detaining the Japanese Americans have been rather closely followed; at least one

[20] Morton Grodzins, *Americans Betrayed* (Chicago: University of Chicago Press, 1949), p. 374.

of the camps used for them in the 1940s was prepared for subversives in the 1950s. More than thirty years ago Sinclair Lewis wrote a sensational novel, *It Can't Happen Here,* about fascism coming to America. As far as one of the chief trappings of most fascist (and communist) regimes is concerned, it has happened here already. Whether or not it will happen again—something we will treat in the concluding chapter—is clearly a matter of conjecture. It is a fact, however, that we now have enabling legislation that makes it much easier, from a technical point of view, for it to happen again.

The Filipinos

Filipinos were the last group of Asians to come to California. Filipino immigration had many characteristics in common with the Chinese and Japanese immigration that preceded it. It was a largely male immigration and the young men who came filled the niche in the labor force that had been occupied by the Japanese, who, by the 1920s, were no longer available in significant numbers to work for Caucasian growers. Had Japanese immigration not been cut off, it is probable that the Filipino migration would not have been as large as it was. The Filipino, however, thanks to American imperialism, enjoyed a different status from other Asians. Like them, Filipinos were not eligible for naturalization; but, since the United States owned the Philippines, they were not aliens, but nationals. As such, Filipinos traveled under United States passports and could not be excluded from the United States. Congress eventually rectified this situation by passing, in 1935, the Tydings-McDuffie Act which granted a deferred independence to the Philippines but imposed immediately a rigid quota of fifty immigrants a year, thus' ending, for all practical purposes, Filipino immigration. Ironically, some of the leading anti-Filipino nativists in California were among the chief advocates of Philippine independence, since independence, or to be precise the promise of independence, was the *sine qua non* of exclusion.

The major thrust of Filipino immigration lasted about ten years. In 1920 there had been only 5,000 Filipinos in the entire country (3,000 in California); by the next census the figures had risen to 45,000 nationwide, with about 30,000 in California. Yet this tiny minority raised the hackles of the California exclusionists, who saw the Filipinos as yet another Asian horde about to overwhelm Caucasian California. A Sacramento exclusionist informed a national magazine audience that since all American Negroes were descended from a small slave nucleus, even this tiny group represented a danger. Ignoring the fact that very few women came from the Philippines, he insisted, with that mindless arithmetic that California exclusionists delighted in, that "Filipinos do not hesitate to have nine children . . . [which means] 729 great-grandchildren as against the white parents' twenty-seven." [21]

But the explosive nature of the Filipino problem was caused not by Filipino reproduction, but by Filipino sex. The sex bugaboo, the ravishing of pure white women by lascivious Oriental men, had always lurked in the background of the anti-Oriental movements in California. It had never become, overtly at least, a major factor for the simple reason that sex relations between Oriental men and Occidental women had been all but nonexistent. (Intercourse between males of the majority race and females of the minority races aroused little opposition; Chinese and Japanese prostitutes had been a titillating feature of west coast brothels since gold-rush days.) With the Filipinos, however, the sex issue became tangible. The Filipinos sought and enjoyed the companionship of Caucasian girls, and soon in every major center of Filipino population in the state, special dance halls sprung up which catered exclusively to the Filipino trade, and a lucrative trade it was. The basic charge was ten cents a minute and such places did a thriving business.

This kind of "free enterprise" was just too much for most Californians. The conservative *Los Angeles Times* railed against two dance halls located just a few blocks from the newspaper's headquarters. One set of headlines read:

> Taxi-Dance Girls Start Filipinos on Wrong Foot
>
> Lonely Islanders' Quest for Woman Companionship Brings Problems of Grave National Moment
>
> Mercenary Women Influence Brown Man's Ego
>
> Minds Made Ripe for Work of Red Organizers

Exclusionists suffered a further shock when the courts ruled that the state's miscegenation statute—which forbade marriages of white

[21] C. M. Goethe, "Filipino Immigration Viewed as a Peril," *Current History* (January 1934), p. 354.

persons with Negroes, Mongolians, or mulattoes—did not apply to the Filipinos, who were adjudged Malayans. The California legislature quickly amended the law to extend the ban to "members of the Malay race." In the meantime the alleged sexual aggressiveness of the Filipinos had set off a good deal of mob violence. (It could be argued that the Filipinos were merely conforming to the "melting pot" ideal, and thus were more Americanized than other Orientals, but this possibility never occurred to California exclusionists.) In addition, the Filipinos, who were often, they felt, exploited by Japanese and Chinese businessmen in the United States, were much more prone to join unions and participate in strikes than earlier Asian immigrants had been, a propensity that caused them to be viewed with alarm in the America of Harding, Coolidge, and Hoover. Despite their willingness to be organized, the California trade union hierarchy wanted little to do with them and participated almost as eagerly in the anti-Filipino movement as it had in previous anti-Oriental crusades.

In short, an unhappy Filipino story in California can be summed up in an aphorism: "last imported, least upwardly mobile." But perhaps it would be best to leave our last word on the subject to Carlos Bulosan, himself a Filipino immigrant and trade union organizer. In his moving autobiography, *America Is in the Heart*, he describes what it felt like to be a Filipino in California in the 1920s:

> . . . in many ways it was a crime to be a Filipino in California. I came to know that the public streets were not free to my people; we were stopped each time . . . patrolmen saw us driving a car. We were suspect each time we were seen with a white woman. And perhaps it was this narrowing of our life into an island, into a filthy segment of American society, that had driven [many] Filipinos inward, hating everyone and despising all positive urgencies toward freedom.[22]

The Mexican American 1910–1940

From the American conquest in 1848 until about 1910, very few Mexicans migrated into California, or into the United States

[22] Carlos Bulosan, *America is in the Heart* (New York: Harcourt, Brace & World, Inc., 1943), p. 220. For a recent evaluation see J. M. Saniel, ed., *The Filipino Exclusion Movement, 1927–1935*, Occasional Papers #1 (Quezon City, Philippines: University of the Philippines, 1967).

for that matter. The relative ease of entry across a long, sparsely-settled border, the difficulty in distinguishing between Spanish-speaking native-born citizens and Spanish-speaking immigrants, and the dubious character of much of the official data, make precise quantification impossible, but the official census and immigration figures are of some use.

IMMIGRATION OF MEXICANS TO THE U.S.

to 1900	28,000
1901–1910	50,000
1911–1920	219,000
1921–1930	460,000
1931–1940	22,000
1941–1950	59,000
1951–1960	319,000

The basic rhythm is easy to explain. Both the "pull" and the "push" increased strongly after 1910 as improved transportation facilities and an expanding economy in the American Southwest (Arizona, California, Colorado, New Mexico, and Texas), and the turmoil caused by the Mexican Revolution, greatly increased the flow of population northward. Although a few of those who came were political refugees of high socioeconomic status and a conservative political bent (General Victoriano Huerta, president of Mexico from 1913 to 1914, died in Texas), the overwhelming majority were poor peasants and city dwellers seeking peace and economic opportunity. As the Spanish-speaking population of the country grew it remained highly localized, with almost 90 percent of it located in the five southwestern states. Not surprisingly California's relative share of this population steadily increased, as the following table shows.

Year	Census definition	Total U.S.	Total Calif.	% in Calif.
1910	"Mexicans of foreign-born and mixed parentage"	382,002	51,037	13.4
1920	"Mexicans of foreign-born and mixed parentage"	731,559	86,610	17.4
1930	"Mexicans"	1,282,883	368,013	29.3
1940	"Spanish mother tongue"	1,570,740	416,140	32.9
1950	"Spanish surname"	2,281,710	591,540	35.8
1960	"Spanish surname"	3,464,999	1,141,207	40.1

Thus, by 1930, the Mexican Americans had become the largest ethnically identifiable minority within the state, a position they retain today. In California their initial economic opportunity was largely agricultural. The steady decline in the number of Japanese and Chinese in the agricultural labor force, plus the wartime manpower shortages of World War I, and the ever-growing need for "stoop labor" in what Carey McWilliams has so aptly dubbed the state's "factories in the field," provided the major source of employment for the Mexican immigrants and their descendants. The 1920 harvest, for the first time, saw Mexican labor predominate. By 1930, a special investigating committee established by conservative Republican Governor C. C. Young declared that the Mexican

> is today a principal source of farm labor in California. . . . He does tasks that white workers will not or cannot do. He works under . . . conditions that are often too trying for white workers. He will work in gangs. He will work under direction, taking orders and suggestions.

As the above indicates, the Mexican seemed, to the California power structure, to be the ideal answer to the state's agricultural needs. A docile, steady laborer who "knew his place"; a laborer who could be replaced easily; a laborer who neither created serious international problems nor raised the hackles of organized labor. When, in the lean years of the 1930s, many Mexican Americans in California cities begin to appear on the relief rolls, "voluntary" programs of repatriation were organized by various California governmental bodies. Los Angeles county, for example, with the cooperation of the federal government, shipped whole trainloads of Mexicans and Mexican Americans back to Mexico. Although there are no reliable figures for repatriation, probably more Mexicans crossed the border heading south during the depression years than came north.

The Mexicans, citizen and alien, who remained in California, lived a segregated, second-class existence. But their segregation was enforced by custom rather than by statute or ordinance. Although some Mexicans, along with more militant Filipinos, were involved in a few abortive agricultural strikes in the 1930s, particularly in the Imperial Valley area, there were no major incidents of ethnic antagonism. As the United States moved from the economic stringency of the great depression to the relative prosperity of the World

War II era, California's Mexican Americans seemed content in an almost somnambulant torpor.

The Negro to 1940

If the Mexican Americans seemed almost irrationally content, the seeming contentment of California's small Negro population was understandable. They were, relatively speaking, quite well off, if any group of American Negroes could be said to be well off in an America that recognized Jim Crow in law as well as in fact. In the first place, there were very few Negroes in California at any time before World War II, despite the fact that in the Spanish period, Negroes had been members of some of the earliest exploring parties and had been among the first non-Indian permanent residents. At the opening of the twentieth century, there were only about 10,000 Negroes in the whole state; by 1940 there were over 100,000, but even these increased numbers represented less than two percent of the state's population.

Although they lived in pocket ghettoes, California's Negroes were clearly not on the bottom of the ethnic ladder in California. In terms both of hostility directed against them and of positive sociopolitical achievement, the Negroes in the state were better off than the Orientals and the Mexican Americans. In Los Angeles, for example, a Negro, Frederick M. Roberts, was elected to the state legislature as early as 1918 (he was re-elected seven times) from a district that initially included more Caucasian than Negro voters. Roberts was a Republican, with ties to the most conservative faction of that party and to certain Negro insurance companies for whom he was the legislative spokesman. In the early twentieth century at least, Negroes went to unsegregated schools in California and no discriminatory legislation was even contemplated by the legislature.

None of the above is to suggest that in this era Californians were less racially prejudiced than other Americans, but rather to point out that the presence of more "threatening" ethnic groups tended to "promote'" the status of less threatening groups, just as the presence of Orientals in nineteenth-century California had promoted all white men, even Catholics and Jews. California Negroes tended to regard themselves as superior, as more American than less Americanized ethnic groups like Orientals or Mexican Americans. (The latter groups reciprocated this somewhat muted antagonism. Mexican Americans delighted in pointing out that they were officially "white," while Japanese explicitly repudiated any linking of Orientals with Negroes. When, in 1941, the West Coast Japanese were interned, a tiny tremor of delight ran through the Negro community.)

Migrants from the Dust Bowl

We could write briefly of other colored ethnic groups in California in the years before World War II, chiefly the East Indians (Californians called them Hindus, but actually most of the less than 10,000 who came were Sikhs), but this would add little if anything to our analysis. It might be much more useful to point out that, during the depression years at least, one other identifiable group was treated as if it were colored: the pitiful refugees from the American dust bowl, the "Okies" and "Arkies" whose story was told so movingly by John Steinbeck in *The Grapes of Wrath*. That these despised migrants were almost to a man white, Anglo-Saxon Protestants, merely adds to the irony of the situation. California in general and Los Angeles in particular reacted with extreme hysteria to this invasion from within. Migrants were arbitrarily excluded from schools, harassed by police and despised by the populace. The city and county of Los Angeles went so far as to set up border patrol stations as far away as the California-Oregon border in an illegal attempt to inhibit internal migration by American citizens. We suspect that this mistreatment of unfortunate people was particularly easy for Californians, since a variegated discrimination had been so integral a part of California life for so long. To further complicate the picture, it should be noted that these southern and southwestern migrants were soon assimilated and themselves injected an additional dose of anti-Negro prejudice into the California environment. Saul Alinsky, the radical organizer, has argued, only partly in jest, that the "Okies and Arkies" and their children, for whom everyone felt so sorry in the 1930s, are today the "worst SOBs in California." Without attempting to validate that obviously subjective reaction, we should point out that, in the 1950s and 60s, this group has added greatly to what is usually known as the "white backlash." As the ethnic history of California makes so clear, being subjected to prejudice does not provide immunity to prejudice.

4

Racism Modified:
World War II and After

World War II represented a crucial and a paradoxical phase in the history of racism, both American and Californian. On the one hand, the United States fought the war with segregated military forces, interned the West Coast Japanese, and had numerous ugly racial incidents in which white majority mob violence was directed at Negroes in Detroit, in New York City, and in other localities, and at Mexican Americans in Los Angeles. On the other hand, a war against racist Nazi Germany produced untold official condemnations of racism, while many federal, state, and local officials gave at least lip service to the ideal of racial equality. In addition, pressure from quasi-militant organizations like the NAACP and A. Phillip Randolph's *ad hoc* "March on Washington" coalition forced minor but significant concessions from a not always reluctant officialdom. It seems clear, in retrospect, that much of the "preparation" for the *volte-face* on segregation that was to occur when the Supreme Court handed down *Brown v. Board of Education,* in May of 1954, was accomplished during the war years.

The Mexican American Awakening

But if the national ethnic picture was one of gradual amelioration, in California new racial and ethnic tensions arose. The tem-

73

porary removal of the most feared minority, the Japanese, seems to have done little to calm California's jangled racial nerves. On the heels of the expulsion of the Issei and their children, the long-smoldering antagonisms between Mexican Americans and the Anglo Americans became open conflict for the first time in the twentieth century. This antagonism can be seen most clearly in two discrete incidents in Los Angeles in 1942 and in 1943—the "Sleepy Lagoon" murder case and the "Zoot Suit" riots.

The "Sleepy Lagoon" murder (the press invented the romantic title; the scene of the crime was actually an abandoned gravel pit) took place on the night of August 1-2, 1942.[1] The victim was a young Mexican American, Jose Díaz, apparently slain as the result of intra-ethnic gang rivalry. Throughout that summer there had been an artificial "crime wave" fabricated by the press and local law enforcement officers, a crime wave allegedly of Mexican-American origin. When the press made a sensation of Díaz's murder, not ordinarily the kind of case to attract press notice, the police followed suit with a mass round-up of suspects. Some twenty-four youths were arrested for the murder and seventeen of them were actually indicted for murder. There was no tangible evidence against any of them but, nevertheless, the local authorities embarked on the largest mass trial for murder ever held in the United States. The defendants were beaten by police, were forced to appear disheveled in court (for a time they were not even allowed to have their hair cut), and eventually, after a long trial, nine were convicted of second degree murder and the other eight found guilty of lesser crimes. What made this seemingly routine homicide significant—although no mention of it can be found in either of the major college texts on California—was the flagrantly illegal behavior of local law enforcement officers, the way in which it revealed certain stark aspects in the existence of California's largest ethnic minority, and because the defense of its victims marks a nodal point in group consciousness and the first "victory" of the Hispanic community over the Anglo Establishment.

The hostility of local law enforcement practices to the Mexican-American population was of long duration, and, as we have seen, was congruent with the California tradition. Innumerable instances

[1] Much of the material in this section is drawn from a UCLA honors thesis by my 'former student, James S. Dimitroff, "The 1942 Sleepy Lagoon Murder: Catalyst for Mexican-American Militancy in Los Angeles," 1968.

of prejudice could be cited, but perhaps most illuminating are the following excerpts from a report given to the Los Angeles County Grand Jury by the Sheriff's department "expert" on Mexican-American behavior, Captain E. Duran Ayres. After presenting rather fanciful statistics on ethnicity and crime—the official taxonomy was black, yellow, and red for Negro, Oriental, and Mexican—Captain Ayres embarked on a historio-sociological account of the Mexican in California. "Mexicans," he reported accurately enough,

> are restricted in the main only to certain kinds of labor, and that being the lowest paid. It must be admitted that they are discriminated against and have been heretofore practically barred from learning trades. . . . This has been very much in evidence in our defense plants, in spite of President Roosevelt's instructions to the contrary. . . . Discrimination and segregation . . . in certain restaurants, public swimming plunges, public parks, theatres, and even in schools, cause resentment among the Mexican people. . . . There are certain parks in the state in which a Mexican may not appear, or else only on a certain day of the week. There are certain plunges where they are not allowed to swim, or else only on one day of the week [and that invariably just prior to cleaning and draining], and it is made evident by signs reading . . . "Tuesdays reserved for Negroes and Mexicans" . . . All of this [and much more] applies to both the foreign and American-born Mexicans.

But Ayres followed this narrative with a blatantly racist explanation for Mexican-American crime and delinquency, an explanation apparently accepted by the Grand Jury and most of the press and probably most of the population.

> . . . the Caucasian [and] especially the Anglo-Saxon, when engaged in fighting . . . resort[s] to fisticuffs . . . ; but this Mexican element considers [good sportsmanship] to be a sign of weakness, and all he knows and feels is a desire to use a knife or some other lethal weapon. In other words, his desire is to kill, or at least let blood. That is why it is difficult for the Anglo-Saxon to understand the psychology of the Indian or even the Latin, and it is just as difficult for the Indian or Latin to understand the psychology of the Anglo-Saxon or those from northern Europe. When there is added to this inborn characteristic that has come down through the ages, the use of liquor, then we certainly have crimes of violence.

Happily, not all the Anglo majority accepted this lesson in "sociology" and under the leadership of writer Carey McWilliams, one of the pioneers of ethnic justice in modern California, a Sleepy Lagoon Defense Committee was formed and fought the case to a successful conclusion. More than two years after the crime—which remains unsolved—the California District Court of Appeals unanimously reversed all the convictions. The subsequent release of the defendants from San Quentin prison was an occasion for rejoicing among their compatriots. In the meantime, however, an even more explosive episode had occurred: the "Zoot Suit" riots.

These riots, in the late spring of 1943, have been largely ignored by historians, but when they are discussed, distortions imply that the young Mexican Americans were the aggressors. For instance, A. A. Hoehling, in *Home Front, U.S.A.* (1966), writes:

> . . . the zoot-suiters of Los Angeles . . . were predominantly Mexican youths with some Negro disciples, between the ages of sixteen and twenty. They wore absurdly long coats with padded shoulders, porkpie hats completed by a feather in the back, watch chains so long they almost touched the ground, and peg-top trousers tapering to narrow cuffs. . . . At best, as one pundit observed, they were "not characterized primarily by intellect." They formed themselves into bands with flamboyant names: the "Mateo Bombers," "Main Street Zooters," "The Califa," "Sleepy Lagooners," "The Black Legion," and many more. Their targets for physical harm were members of the armed forces, with a special predilection for sailors. The latter fought back with devastating effect. The situation quickly deteriorated to the point that the Navy declared Los Angeles out of bounds. The city council outlawed the wearing of zoot suits for the duration and the city simmered down.

This account, more fantasy than fact, faithfully summarizes what Hoehling read in the newspapers. The facts of the matter are that after certain clashes between sailors on pass or leave (not generally the most decorous group in the population) and civilian teen-agers, the sailors, with the tacit approval of both the naval authorities and the police, made organized assaults not just on zoot suiters who were a tiny fraction of Mexican-American youth, but upon any Mexican they could catch. Carey McWilliams, in *North From Mexico*, describes one organized foray in which "about two hundred sailors" hired "a fleet of twenty taxicabs" and cruised around town beating up Mexicans in ones and twos.[2] After receiving accolades from the press—"Sailor Task Force Hits L. A. Zooters"—the servicemen came out in even greater force the next night; the police, although forewarned, did little if anything to inhibit the violence against Mexicans, although they did arrest twenty-seven Mexican youths. For several nights the streets of Los Angeles were turned over to informal "posses" of servicemen who proceeded to beat, strip and otherwise humiliate every Mexican American (and some Negroes) they could find. Bars were wrecked, movie theaters invaded, all with the same kind of impunity once granted to vigilantes in San Francisco. Throughout it all, the press made it appear that the Mexican-American youths were the aggressors rather than the victims, with headlines like:

> 44 Zooters Jailed in Attacks on Sailors
>
> Zoot Suit Chiefs Girding for War on Navy
>
> Zoot Suiters Learn Lesson in Fight with Servicemen

An exception to this biased coverage was a small community paper, *The Eastside Journal,* which published accurate eyewitness accounts by reporter Al Waxman. He describes coming upon

> a band of servicemen making a systematic tour of East First Street [in the heart of the main Mexican quarter]. They had just come out of a cocktail bar where four men were nursing bruises. Three autos loaded with Los Angeles policemen were on the scene but the soldiers were not molested. Farther down the street the men stopped a streetcar, forcing the motorman to open the door and proceeded to inspect the clothing of the male passengers. . . .

When Waxman pleaded with local police to put a stop to these activities, they answered that it was a matter for the military police. But the local police themselves contributed positively to the disorder. Again quoting reporter Waxman:

> Four boys came out of a pool hall. They were wearing the zoot suits that have become the symbol of a fighting flag. Police ordered them into arrest cars. One refused. He asked, "Why am I being arrested?" The police officer answered with three swift blows of the night-stick across the boy's head and he went down.

[2] Carey McWilliams, *North From Mexico* (Philadelphia, Pa.: J. B. Lippincott Co., 1949), pp. 244–58.

As he sprawled, he was kicked in the face. . . . At the next corner, a Mexican mother cried out, "Don't take my boy, he did nothing. He's only fifteen years old. Don't take him." She was struck across the jaw and almost dropped [her] baby.

If they had not already known, Sleepy Lagoon and the Zoot Suit riots made it crystal clear to California's Mexican population just how second class their citizenship was. At the same time that the community's elder sons were dying on foreign battlefields, some of the younger ones were casualties in their own neighborhoods. Before these wartime incidents, a paternalistic myth somewhat obscured the existing relationships between the Mexicans and their Anglo neighbors; from that time until the present day, the paternalistic relationship has been more and more resented.

Despite its lingering resentment, the Mexican-American community has not been nearly as militant as has the Negro community. The reasons for the relative lack of protest are many, but surely major among them have been the lack of unity among California's Mexican population, the lack of aggressive leadership from within the community, and, perhaps most important of all, an entirely different cultural tradition, one which does not encourage the young to strive in "approved Protestant ethic" fashion. Contemporary census data show this quite clearly. The 1960 figures show that only 8.8 percent of "Spanish surname" males and 6.2 percent of "Spanish surname" females had as much as one year of college, a figure far lower than that for any other ethnic group in California. Since the late 1960s Mexican-American protests over inadequate schooling in their neighborhoods, the appearance of a militant group called the "Brown Berets," a growing insistence on bi-cultural education, and heightened political consciousness among Hispanic groups throughout the whole Southwest, suggest that only in the sixties was the quiescent period coming to an end. By the sixties, also, California-born Mexican leadership was beginning to assert itself. In Los Angeles, the Mexicans have long had a congressman, Edward Roybal, and have recently elected Harvard-trained historian Julian Nava to the school board. But the most impressive leadership has developed in the quasi-feudal central valley where Caesar Chavez has done the impossible by creating a viable trade union of migrant and semi-migrant agricultural workers. His farm workers' union, formerly independent but now affiliated with the AFL-CIO, has managed to unite two previously hostile ethnic groups, the Mexicans, who comprise the majority of the union, and the Filipinos. Chavez skillfully combines the techniques of the modern trade union leader—he has a flair for publicity and has managed to fight off a Teamster raid—with that of an early Mexican religious revolutionary—to surmount one union crisis he endured a lengthy fast. Yet by all the measurable indices, group consciousness among the Spanish-speaking minority in this country is far below that of the black community. The Spanish-speaking community both admires and deprecates the heightened Negro militance, and clearly, from an objective point of view, an alliance between the groups, in the Southwest at least, would be of mutual advantage. Outside observers, like Gunnar Myrdal, posit the existence of an "underclass" in America, and they assume that a united front of the oppressed is actually in existence. These observers underestimate the jealousies and hostilities that exist between the various groups. Mexican Americans in the past were quick to point out that they were white and would pull out driver's licenses to prove it, while many Negroes have assumed the majority prejudice against "spiks." Members of each group are convinced that the "power structure" favors the other group to the disadvantage of their own. Mexican Americans on the one hand, point out that "we don't riot," while on the other hand they bewail the fact (to them) that Negroes get rewards for their disorder, while they get little for their orderliness.

The "New" Oriental

If the Mexican Americans are California's most numerous minority, Orientals are currently the most successful, the most middle-class, the most respected and the least feared and resented. That this became true less than a generation after Pearl Harbor and the relocation, is a change in opinion and mores the magnitude of which is not yet appreciated by most students of social change. There was an abortive "don't let the Japs come back" campaign, but it secured very little support. Many, if not most Californians, seemed to be aware that the evacuation of 1942 had been unnecessary. At any rate, most of the Japanese did come back, and although there were a few ugly incidents, most of those who returned managed to pick up at least some of the pieces of their shattered lives. That they were allowed to do so may in part be due to the fact that other minority problems "promoted" the Japanese, but high among the causal components of this change is the very real achievement of the Japanese Americans of the second and third generation, not to speak of the pioneering efforts of the Issei themselves. To put it in a nutshell, the Japanese Americans—and to a slightly lesser degree the Chinese Americans—have become more white than the majority, if by white we mean highly educated, middle-class persons. Despite all these achievements, however, the census data demonstrate conclusively that Chinese and Japanese are still discriminated against. This discrimination shows most clearly in the education and income data. It is a good rule of thumb that they go hand in hand in our materialistic, technological society. For Orientals here, this is only a half-truth. Although California's Chinese and Japanese are better educated than California's white population, they do not have the income usually associated with advanced education. Although college graduates are 11 percent more likely to be found among Japanese males than among white males, and 24 percent more frequent among Chinese males, white men make considerably more money. For every $51 received by a white Californian, Japanese get $43 and Chinese $38. If we look at the very well off, the imbalance is even greater. A white man's chances of achieving an annual income of $10,000 or more are 78 percent better than those of a Chinese and 57 percent better than those of a Japanese.

Along with their middle-class achievements, Japanese and Chinese have picked up middle-class values. When Negroes move into Oriental neighborhoods, the Orientals often flee to the suburbs. Some Japanese leaders have publicly lectured Negroes to follow their example, and have managed on occasion to sound as unsympathetic to Negro aspirations as Mayor Daley or Louise Day Hicks. Yet, at the same time, on the leadership level at least, there have been some faltering steps toward a united front of all disadvantaged and ethnic groups. During the 1964 campaign to defeat the anti-fair-housing ordinance, Proposition 14 (we will discuss this in more detail later), an impressive roster of Oriental and Mexican-American leaders issued a joint statement supporting the position taken by the Negro community and shared with white liberals. But an examination of voting in technically identifiable wards shows the rank and file less amenable to unity than the leadership. (The same holds true of the identifiable Jewish vote.)

The Negro

If the Orientals in California have become more white since World War II, the Negro in California has become more black; the "promotion" of some other minorities has thrust the Negro to the bottom rung of the ethnic ladder, his traditional position in American society. This change in relative position in California has come about not only through the promotion of other groups, but also because the increasing number of Negroes and their concentration in explosive ghettoes have made them seem a threat to other groups in society. While the war served as an excuse for expelling the Japanese and exacerbating the tensions between Mexican Americans and Anglos, it also served as a magnet drawing Negroes to California, along with millions of others. California was transformed into a major industrial state by the demands for planes, ships, and other military hardware. It became the major staging area for the Pacific Theater in World War II and for the Korean and Viet Nam conflicts. California's Negro population almost quadrupled between 1940 and 1950 and nearly doubled in the next decade. The 1960 census found nearly 900,000 Negroes who represented about six percent of the population. Negroes were, by 1960, the second largest minority group in the state. More vigorous politically and more militant than any of the other groups and clustered into ghettoes of varying quality in Los Angeles, Oakland-Berkeley and San Francisco, they have been able to exercise more political clout than the more numerous Mexicans. In addition to a Congressman, Augustus Hawkins of Los Angeles, they have been able to elect Negroes to both houses of the state legislature and to local governing boards throughout the state. These and other tangible indications of progress allowed fantasy-prone California officials to assert that no significant discrimination existed in California. Two events of the mid-sixties—the 1964 election on a fair-housing proposition and the 1965 Watts riots—managed to dispel that chimera as events of the forties had shattered the myth of the happy Mexican.

The anti-fair-housing proposition on the ballot in 1964 was actually an attempt to repeal an existing and not too effective state fair-housing statute, the so-called Rumford Act. The proposition on the ballot (Proposition 14) was so worded that it not only repealed the

Rumford Act but also put a bar against future fair-housing statutes into the state constitution. (This, of course, made it unconstitutional, as most legal experts foresaw and the courts have since ruled.) The proposition was sponsored by real estate groups and was hedged with statements about the rights of individuals to dispose of their own property as they saw fit. It was, in fact, a statewide referendum on racism. Apart from marriage, housing is probably the most sensitive area in American race relations. The people of California, by about 3 to 2, voted against fair housing. This open rejection of integration in housing (symbolic rejection, of course—most Negroes do not have the means to move into white neighborhoods even if they have the inclination) was not without influence in the worsening of Negro-white relations in the months that followed.

The other event, the Watts riots of August 11–17, 1965, probably marks a watershed in Negro-white relations, not just in California but in the whole country. Watts was not the first riot—there had been serious disturbances in seven Eastern cities the summer before—but it was the first that appeared to have the character of a rebellion. Perhaps the most surprising thing about the riot was that it happened in Los Angeles, which, only the previous year, had been ranked by the National Urban League as the most favorable to Negroes of the 68 American cities examined. Although the riots have been widely studied, there is no consensus of opinion among its students; however, the basic facts are reasonably clear.

On the evening of August 11, 1965, the Negro ghetto of Los Angeles erupted with outbreaks of mob violence at first centered near, but not in, a small area known as Watts, but soon it spread over much of a vast ghetto. Set off by a seemingly routine arrest of a drunken driver, it resulted in 144 hours of anarchic looting, arson, assault, and homicide. This happened in an area with supposedly exemplary race relations. More than half the Negro population of the state lives in Los Angeles county (461,000 enumerated by the 1960 census), most of it in the overcrowded south Los Angeles ghetto that sprawls over 50 square miles. The housing there was (and remains) substandard. It consists of one- and two-story single and multi-family structures, most of which have at least the hint of a lawn. About half were built before World War II, which is a very long time ago as far as Los Angeles housing is concerned. Many of these units, however, are sound and well-maintained. These atypical ghetto conditions made it possible for civic leaders (including some Negro leaders) to insist that the city had no real race relations problem, a kind of dream state peculiarly appropriate to a region that boasts of Hollywood and Disneyland. Similar wishful thinking prevailed in the same quarters during much of the Great Depression, when local leaders tried to maintain that Los Angeles was the economic "white spot" of the nation. Reality finally punctured both illusions; both however, like most illusions, had some basis in reality. As bad as conditions were for the white émigrés of the 1930s—think of Steinbeck's Joads—and are for the Negro newcomers now, they are distinctly better than the conditions they left behind. But in all too many instances these conditions have not lived up to the expectations of the new arrivals, and it is these partially thwarted expectations that have made California, and other northern and western "promised lands," sociological and political powder kegs, with a markedly lower burning point than the objective conditions within them might suggest.

If the Watts riots seem similar to earlier ethnic violence, that similarity is largely superficial. The most obvious difference is that the earlier violence had been that of a majority directed against a particular minority. The Watts riots—and similar events in other cities—saw a minority, really a small minority of a minority, lash out blindly against the society which, in their opinion, was oppressing them intolerably. (Historically it would probably be more accurate to suggest that society was not easing its restrictions as fast as expectations were rising.) Another difference is that these riots were largely directed against property, and quite often Negro-owned and occupied property. The aggression was almost all Negro, and so, ironically, have been most of the victims.

The foundation for Watts and other riots—apart from mimesis after Watts—is a simple one: an alienated group squeezed into a small ghetto. Within that group there are growing numbers (almost all the estimates are too small) of under-educated, under-skilled and therefore unemployed youths in the nation with the greatest educational system in the world. In Los Angeles the ghetto is not an area of abject poverty—about 60 percent of the population get some kind of welfare and California standards are, relatively speaking, quite high—but one of apathy, resentment, and hopelessness. These ingredients were detonated in Los Angeles by a casual incident which resulted in an opportunity for some to lash back at society in general and the police in particular, and gave many more a chance for vicarious pleasure in merely watching them do it.

That this widespread alienation exists so noticeably at a time when Negroes seem to be making such great strides, has puzzled and perplexed many, but it should be quite clear that although the social revolution that John Kenneth Galbraith has dubbed "affluence" has affected the American Negro, north and south, not nearly enough of it has trickled down. But within the same society that sees many Negroes achieving upward social mobility and a few grasping political and economic power, there are within most Negro communities large numbers of socially alienated young men and women, children of the welfare state at its worst, who have neither known extreme economic deprivation nor ever experienced a normal family life. They have not even been able to indulge in the humblest aspect of the American Dream, *the reasonable expectation that their children would have a chance to better themselves.* These people carried through and enjoyed the Los Angeles riots and the many similar incidents that followed.

Like the Mexican Americans before them, the Negroes in California have charged that the governmental establishment and in particular the law enforcement agencies are prejudiced against them, and often the cry of police brutality is heard. Although standards among police forces in the state naturally vary—Oakland is probably the worst, Los Angeles the best—old-fashioned police brutality with rubber hoses, cattle prods and police dogs simply does not exist, although the club will be wielded and the pistol unholstered much quicker in a black community than in a white one. What do exist in California are police forces which, in a thousand ways, small and large, harass Negroes and subject them to constant indignities. This is merely another natural byproduct of the racism that is so much a part of the American way of life; it is not official policy.

Since Watts, ghetto violence has become a commonplace; the long hot summer with burning, looting, and federal troops has occurred with sickening regularity. Violence has spilled over into the political and educational process; extremism of all kinds seems to be proliferating at every level of society. Clearly not all of this violence is attributable solely to our racial malaise, but there is little of it that is not somehow related. This racism, as we have seen, has been a major thread of the American experience from the very first, and it would take a foolish optimist indeed to expect it to disappear in the foreseeable future. But if the California experience means anything, it seems to mean that racism is a variable and not the absolute that fashion tends to make it. Targets and intensity can and do change, sometimes with almost stupefying rapidity. No scrutiny of the past can make a realistic observer sanguine about our immediate racial and ethnic future, but it can give him some hope for the days ahead.

5

Boundary Maintenance

We began by assuming a simple two-category stratification system which, like most ideal models, violates somewhat issues which are infinitely complex; nevertheless, the historical data suggest that a two-category model is, in fact, the most suitable. Two simple categories, white and nonwhite seem to dominate the social structure, and the color barrier seems to have been the single most important factor in determining white and nonwhite relationships.

The view of the "outsider," be he Indian, Chinese, Japanese, Filipino, Mexican, or Negro, can be summed up by the Filipino, Bulosan, in his autobiographical novel in which he describes a grievance meeting of his countrymen in California.

> "How come we Filipinos in California can't buy or lease real estate?" a man asked.
>
> "Why are we denied civil service jobs?" asked another.
>
> "Why can't we marry women of the Caucasian race? And why are we not allowed to marry in this state?"
>
> "Why can't we practice law?"
>
> "Why are we denied the right to becoming naturalized American citizens?"
>
> "Why are we discriminated against in relief agencies?"

"Why are we denied better housing conditions?"

"Why can't we stop the police from handling us like criminals?"

"Why are we denied recreational facilities in public parks and other places?" [1]

And each member of a target group could add his queries to the list. Why was insurance so hard to get? Why were swimming pools so difficult to integrate? Why was restaurant service so slow? Why did one have to be "better" in order to hold a job?

But the questioning of barriers, be they social, economic, or political, is apparently not a simple, randomized procedure. Instead, they reflect on ordering which provides an interesting commentary on distorted perceptions, since the views of the white and the nonwhite emphasize a different set of priorities.

For example, Myrdal,[2] in analyzing white discriminatory practices, hypothesizes the following rank order. The gravest fear of the majority relates to intermarriage and sexual intercourse across color lines, so that the whole area of preventing intimate social interaction ranks as the highest priority. Other social forms also rank high—taboos on dancing and drinking together—as rules of dominant to inferior relationships.

The use of public facilities is not viewed as strictly by the whites, therefore integrated eating places, schools, churches, and parks are of medium rank in terms of boundary maintenance. And perhaps the easiest boundaries to overcome relate to areas such as political disenfranchisement, discrimination in the law courts, police practices, the securing of credit, purchasing land, job opportunity, and applying for public welfare. Although Myrdal's rankings were made several decades ago and certain changes in emphasis have taken place, his general thesis, that boundary maintenance for the majority group is the strictest in the personal areas and relaxes as one reaches the less personal areas, is a valid one.

The minority group is apt to care about overcoming racial boundaries in the reverse order of priority. Dating or marrying white women, or having white friends, seems infinitely less important than finding a good job, being treated fairly by police and judges, and, especially, by teachers and welfare workers. For most nonwhites,

---

[1] Carlos Bulosan, *America Is in the Heart* (New York: Harcourt, Brace & World, Inc., 1943), pp. 268–69.

[2] G. Myrdal, *An American Dilemma* (New York: Harper & Bros., 1944), pp. 60–61.

changes in the economic and political arenas are considered to be of primary importance, though a sequence is envisioned which does include eventual progress to intimate social areas once "success" has been achieved in the others.

Whites and nonwhites, then, see the problems of racial integration in very different, even opposite ways, and these differing perceptions determine the targets of social change. For minorities, representatives of the law, of education, and of social welfare become the primary contacts with whites; accusations of racism are most often raised against police, teachers, and social workers. Since these roles are institutionalized, it is often most difficult to change them, and bigotry can conceal itself in the mountainous red tape and innumerable "regulations" by which these institutions seem to run. To complicate the problem, members of police forces, welfare departments, and so on, are apt to be members of groups who are, or were, recently marginal, and are most threatened by minority behavior in consequence.

That social workers and policemen may come from sub-groups which have recently passed into some sort of social acceptance suggests a further consideration, that the boundary which separates the two parts of a two-category social structure is neither rigid nor impermeable. It is possible to make a number of observations about its configuration; the most general one is that the permeability of the boundary, for each individual and group, will be determined by the group's relationship to the standards set up by the majority community. Color, numbers, nationality, religion, political ideology, culture, and marginality are the factors taken into consideration, but these criteria differ considerably in their relative importance.

Color

Color is the most important determinant of permeability. White skin color explains why the "Okies" of the 1930s have been upwardly mobile and why European immigrant groups have been more successful than those from Asia, Africa, and South America. Among nonwhite groups, degree of pigmentation has had a direct bearing on success. White supremacists usually have a well-developed sense of which races are superior and which are inferior: the rank order precisely corresponds to pigmentation. For example, one common ranking of racial superiority is the following: [3] 1. Caucasian, 2. Mongolian, 3. Malaysian, 4. American Indian, 5. Negro. The lighter the skin pigmentation the higher the status, and even within the Caucasian group the blonde Nordic types are supposedly superior to darker Southern Europeans. Lighter-skinned Orientals have generally been more mobile than the darker Africans. O'Brien [4] notes, for example, that during World War II, Japanese in the racially segregated city of Memphis were buried in the white section of the cemetery. Hitler's white Aryan theories were elastic enough to include the yellow Japanese nation because it was politically and militarily expedient to do so. The economically important Japanese businessman is considered white in South Africa, at least as far as business is concerned.

Several generalizations appear appropriate. First, color of groups and individuals is relative, and those farthest removed from the desired whiteness have a more difficult time permeating the boundaries separating them from the white group. Part of the hostility against Orientals in California in the late 1880s and up through World War II can be explained by the fact that there were so few Negroes in California at the time to constitute any sort of threat, and the Orientals were therefore at the bottom of the color ladder. But even at the height of anti-Oriental agitation, "far-sighted" California politicians warned of a bigger potential race problem if Negroes were to come in large numbers. For the individual Negro, the barriers are nearly universal at present, and perhaps majority group reactions to blackness are more nearly absolute than relative. Therefore, in any color stratification schema involving the Negro, he will tend to be at the bottom, and only if he is absent do the other nonwhite groups occupy basement positions. It may further follow that if all nonwhite groups were removed from the social scheme, the boundaries may be shifted in order to exclude swarthier Caucasians, or, because color is the most important but not the sole determining factor in permeability, perhaps other variables such as religion (the Jew), or social class would become the dominant motive in maintaining stratification.

[3] Stuart Landry, *The Cult of Equality* (New Orleans: Pelican Publishing Co., 1945).

[4] Robert W. O'Brien, "Selective dispersion as a factor in the solution of the Nisei problem," *Social Forces*, XXIII, No. 2, December 1944, 140–47.

Numbers

The size of a group also affects the position and permeability of the boundary excluding it from social acceptance. We can recall the elaborate geometric charts of earlier eras which showed California overrun by yellow hordes. The constant fear among the white group of becoming a numerical minority in any given social or geographical segment of America, is doubtless intensified by the uneasy realization that whites are in fact a numerical minority of the world population.

Colonial experiences have provided certain models for the control of large native populations by a numerically smaller group. After the traditional use of force, other techniques evolved: the employment of native intermediaries, the separation of the numerically larger groups, and the device of "divide and conquer." In California, the "Yellow Peril" was averted by restrictive immigration legislation, effected in Congress through the cooperation of Southern congressmen who understood the issue of racism and the importance of protecting the majority status of the whites.

California fought various other battles to restrain the size of "undesirable" groups. The "Okies," the Mexicans, the hippies, the fear of hordes of destitute and sick flocking in to live on state welfare programs, have all contributed to the slightly paranoid cast of California political psychology. The most obvious consideration about numbers and permeability relates to sheer size. The biggest sub-groups constitute the greatest threat to the boundaries, and therefore the greatest efforts at maintaining them have been and will be directed against such groups. Conversely, groups having very small numbers can permeate the boundary most easily. Our historical data lend validity to this hypothesis: for instance, in California first the Chinese, then the Japanese, and today the Mexican and Negro have replaced each other as primary targets of public fear as they replace each other as large minorities. The numerically small Filipino, Korean, and Hindu groups have never been the primary targets of hostility.

There is probably an optimum size for a minority group. It should be large enough to support some of its own structures and institutions so that it does not have to depend on the larger community for satisfaction of its major needs; but, it should be small enough so that it cannot exist as a completely isolated system out of all contact with the majority culture.

Another consideration, related to numbers, is the geographical distribution of a minority. Permeability is negatively related to large ethnic clusters or ghettoes, and the more concentrated an ethnic group is, the more difficulty its members will have in entering the majority social system.

Nationality

The permeability of boundaries for immigrant groups has often been determined by the relationships between their home-lands and America. Obviously, with fluctuations in international relations, friends may find themselves enemies, or the reverse, in short periods of time. Oddly enough, to have come from an enemy nation is not entirely a disadvantage to the immigrant. For one thing, he probably has come from a nation strong enough to be worth considering inimical, and he may have the support and protection of his government. The Chinese suffered during the early California years, because they did not have the backing of an international power, while the early Japanese profited from the strong Japanese nation during the same period. What happened to this group during World War II, of course, exemplifies the *disadvantages* of coming from an enemy nation.

It is often an asset in everyday life to be a foreigner. Visitors from Africa are usually treated better than American Negroes, for example, and Indians in their turbans fare better than similar dark-skinned people who in ordinary clothes might be taken for members of less desirable minorities. This phenomenon is somewhat deceptive, however, because foreign visitors are apt to represent the more privileged classes of their nations, and therefore may command admiration and civility on other grounds: money, cultivation, accomplishment, and so on.

Religion

Although early attacks on the Chinese indicted their "heathen ways," religion has not generally been an important factor in maintaining separation boundaries. For one thing, most minorities are not religiously unlike the majority group: Mexicans are Catholics, Negroes and Japanese are generally Protestants. No significant American minority represents other than Judeo-Christian religions.

Political Ideology

Like religion, political ideology has not been an important factor in restricting the mobility of nonwhite groups. It is simple to call disliked groups "Communist," "Fascist," "Bolshevik," and so on, but these pejoratives have not been used too often against the nonwhite. Most groups, like the Japanese, have either been apolitical or conservative, and American legislation against minorities has tended to ensure that this remains the case: denial of citizenship or the franchise is the most obvious technique employed. The absence of radical political activity among disadvantaged minority groups has in fact been surprising. Segregated, exploited, these people would have the least to lose and the most to gain from radical change, but, because their own subcultures have been essentially conservative, and because of their desire to be accepted and integrated, they seemed to have preferred not to "rock the boat."

Culture

By this we refer to the institutions and structures developed by sub-groups, and the norms and values they teach. As we have said (pp. 15 ff.), in a social learning model sense, the structures and institutions act as agents, shapers, socializers, and reinforcers; norms and values help determine the content, the direction, and the "how" and "what" of the teaching area. The way a man behaves, how he will communicate and what he expects and values will vary with different cultures and will even differ within the same culture.

The present study cannot analyze any of the many subcultures in detail; instead it will focus upon the interdependent factors that relate to upward mobility, social control, and boundary maintenance. These include the strength and cohesion of the subculture; its relative independence of majority culture boundary maintenance institutions, and the prescriptions of the culture.

The Japanese-American culture is one example of a strong and cohesive group, by which we refer to its power to provide for its own needs. It included intact families for socialization purposes, viable structures and institutions for educational, economic, and moral teaching, and an overall positive ethnic identification. There were jobs within the ethnic community, Japanese language schools and many community organizations available for varying social purposes. There were ethnic churches. There were Japanese newspapers, banks, lending institutions. Above all, the Japanese could identify with a successful, although alternate "opportunity structure," so that when majority group boundary maintenance procedures were rigid, individuals were still able to live a relatively independent existence. If their lives were not as full as could be hoped—and the college graduates manning fruit stands in the 1930s did not augur well for the future of things—there were many Japanese working in banks, hospitals, and businesses, positions that could provide the training necessary for a boundary breakthrough.

Another cultural factor in predicting mobility for a group is its degree of independence from majority group mechanisms designed to preserve its boundaries. Those groups, conversely, who are most dependent on the majority community, are the most susceptible to its exclusion measures; for instance, groups living mainly on public welfare or by menial labor which precludes advancement, promotion, and other means of mobility, have the least chance of overcoming the boundaries of the two-category system.

Finally, those subcultures having norms and values most congruent with WASP expectations will generally permeate boundaries at a higher rate than those having less congruent value systems. Therefore, subcultures which emphasize hard work, high educational achievement, delayed gratification, and large savings accounts will be very much likelier to succeed. Further, if norms for interaction with the larger community are based on accommodation and compatibility rather than confrontation and hostility, the probabilities of upward mobility may be heightened. There are some undoubted advantages to being an Uncle Tom.

Six variables should be considered, then, with regard to the likelihood or speed of the permeation by a subgroup of the majority: those groups with 1. lighter skin color, 2. smaller numbers, 3. compatible nationalities, 4. similar religions, 5. congruent political ideologies, and 6. compatible cultures, are ordinarily most successful with the dominant WASP culture. This is exemplified by the current situation in California where the Orientals, who are the closest to the WASP's on all six variables, are likewise the most acceptable. The most important predictor variables apparently are the interdependence between color and culture.

Other Variables

Several other pyschological variables affecting permeation should also be mentioned. First is the concept of psychological marginality: those with extremely weak ethnic identifications may attempt to become a part of the majority group, and this process may be affected through name change, altering of physiological features, and other attempts to escape the negative image. Also, individuals with unusual talents or abilities may find upward mobility possible. There is also a sex differential; generally, nonwhite females have an easier time than males in crossing the boundaries.

Tilting of the Boundary Line

The tilt of the boundary line in the two-category stratification system is another important factor relating to permeability. There are several ways we can conceive of the boundary line being drawn; obviously, any shift in the position of nonwhites means a shift in the shape of the boundary. The diagrams below illustrate three possible models of two-category systems, and imply, perhaps, a logical evolution among them.

Fig. A	Fig. B	Fig. C

Superior

Inferior

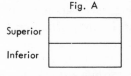

1. Two-category system: all whites "superior" to nonwhites	1. Two-category system: most whites "superior" to nonwhites	1. Two-category system: no group "superior" to the other

Theoretical equality between groups is reached at C, where the boundaries remain, but in such a position as to eliminate superiors and inferiors, and both groups maintain equal economic, social, and political power. This model illustrates what Gordon calls structural pluralism, whereby groups exist separately but side by side. Clear examples of this kind of social organization do not exist in our country, but may presumably be found in a country like Malaysia, where natives, Chinese, and Europeans may retain their own languages, institutions, and cultures and yet live side by side. But even there, the presumed equality of the groups can be questioned.

One reason we in America do not have situations like those in Figure C is illustrated in Figure B, which shows how individual nonwhites may push the boundary, producing a situation in which some nonwhites are superior to some whites. This sets in motion several other processes. As we have previously said, the size and marginality of a group affect its mobility. An upward rise is achieved by only a few nonwhites at a time, and the individuals involved find themselves in a sociologically marginal position. Having risen above most of their own group, they discover that it is easier to find compatible social, intellectual, and marital contacts in the majority rather than in the minority intellectual group. Predictably, many of these individuals leave their own group and integrate into the larger society.

For example, a nonwhite male who achieves a Ph.D. will find himself in a marginal position. He will find few ethnic group cohorts —eventual dating and marital patterns may be across the color line. Or there may be others who find upward mobility and ethnic identification a handicap and dissociate themselves from the ethnic group and attempt to permeate the color line.

Most of our white immigrant groups have gone through the process shown in Figure B. They started on the bottom, somewhat separated from the majority society (but with the important exception of facing no color barrier), gradually losing their national and other identities. As the boundary tilts, those achieving middle- and upper-middle-class status are absorbed into the middle-class American culture and identify as Americans.

But nonwhite subgroups, with similar drives for upward mobility on American identity and integration, have not been as successful because of the color barrier. Instead, they may be closer to model C, although a true pluralism may never take place.

The Major Problem in Summary

The problems of boundary maintenance, permeation, and superiority are aptly summarized by Berry:

The underprivileged minority conceives of the problem as one of achieving a more desirable status, of removing the stigma of inferiority, of casting off the disabilities and handicaps imposed upon it, of acquiring power and status equal to that of any other group. To the dominant group, on the other hand, the race problem is conceived essentially as one of preserving its way of life. A docile, subservient, industrial, racial or ethnic minority can be most useful, and even indispensable; but such a minority becomes a menace when it grows restless, seeks to change its status, and aspires to play new roles.[5]

The white majority group tends to develop an elaborate strategy to maintain the separation of itself and the minority group. Basically, the strategy is simple. Power—political, economic, and educational—must be under its own control. Legislation should systematically lead to the subjugation and deprivation of people in the lower category. Voting, ownership of property, and other means of retaining power should be restricted; schools and other educational opportunities must be separate; occupations should reflect the dichotomy; housing must be segregated and anti-miscegenation laws must guarantee no intermingling ("the mongrelization of the race"). The institutions of social control—the schools, the legal system, the courts, the judges, and the police—are to serve as representatives of the superior group.

As we have demonstrated, these discriminatory practices (Stages 2 and 3) predictably lead to disadvantage, segregation, and isolation. But a two-category system cannot operate easily without an efficient method of assignment—such as outward physical appearance. The basic social roles must have an obligatory character—whites must behave like whites; Negroes must behave like Negroes; Mexicans must behave like Mexicans; Japanese must behave like Japanese and overall, nonwhites must behave like nonwhites. The racial signs are important because they provide a quick and unequivocal classification in a high proportion of circumstances. In most two-category systems, skin complexion and physical appearance are the most overt signs, although Banton[6] mentions that in more physically homogeneous cultures, cues may center on variables

[5] Brewton Berry, *Race and Ethnic Relations* (Boston: Houghton Mifflin Company, 1958), p. 411.
[6] Michael Banton, *Race Relations* (London: Tavistock Publications, 1967), p. 58.

such as the size of the lips, the height of the cheekbones, or the texture of the hair.

However, in actual practice, a two-category system is impossible to enforce. Even in the Deep South, instead of two categories with considerable social distance, the white and Negro categories tend to "fragment into smaller interest groups, distance was reduced, an overlap in status was sometimes apparent, and more mixing occurred." [7]

In California, the introduction of diverse nonwhite populations provides experiences which form the basis for several hypotheses. (We introduce the term hypothesis in the sense of summarizing and guiding our thinking, rather than using it in the sense of final empirical verification.) Our historical data lend support to our perspective.

HYPOTHESIS ONE

If the two-category system is structurally determined, certain predictions can be made. It is the position of the pariah group, not the group itself that is most important. Those nonwhite people at the bottom of the structure will be the target of majority disapprobation regardless of their actual characteristics. All or any pariah group will "breed like rabbits," for example, or "lower property values." Historical data support this hypothesis: for instance, nineteenth-century Englishmen thought these things of the Irish, and conceived of that national group as having darker skin. In California, no group has occupied the lowest rung of the social ladder for long, but each one, while there, has had these characteristics attributed to it. First the Indian, then the Chinese, the Japanese, the "Okie," the Filipino, the Mexican, and now the Negro have displaced each other in the unenvied position. Unfortunately, because color remains the single most important factor in determining discrimination, the relative lightness of the earlier groups gave them upward mobility which may be difficult for darker groups to attain.

A second prediction is that society will tend to support a two-category, rather than a multiple-category system, with the basic boundary determinant, color, being variously defined. When potential third categories appear they are generally dealt with by the majority in such a way as to maintain the dual structure. For ex-

[7] *Ibid.*, p. 126.

ample, Banton, in describing the classification of Indians in Mississippi, found that a third category was resisted because it logically
required building a third set of schools, waiting rooms, and other facilities. There may also be more subtle reasons for maintaining only
two categories. One of the gravest dangers in a three-or-more-cate-
gory system, where one group remains superior, is the realistic fear
within that group of a coalition among the disadvantaged. Members of the superior group find it difficult to maintain this superior
relationship with more than one group at a time. Research on
triadic family relationships invariably shows them resolving into
coalitions of two against one.

Neither can the superior group lump all other groups into one
category such as nonwhite, because this might lead to the eventual
numerical superiority of the nonwhite group. Thus, another prediction is that nonwhite groups who are not primary targets of superior
group hostility will be perceived as "whiter" by the majority, and,
furthermore, they will tend to act "whiter," which may mean acting
with even greater hostility than the majority toward pariah groups.
These things happen in various subgroups within society—for instance within the academic world. There, disciplines often break
themselves down into such dichotomies as "basic" and "applied," or
"scientific" and "nonscientific," and the superior group, which usually
correlates directly to a level of abstractness, looks down on its more
practical colleagues. Within the more "practical group," those who
perceive themselves as closer to science tend to look down on their
less scientific colleagues.

In a two-category system, it is easy to predict that those of more
recent inclusion into the accepted category will "try harder," in the
words of the second-class car renters. That is behavior which most
people understand. It follows from this philosophy that those white
groups which are "less acceptable" as a result of either class and/or
national origins, may also act "whiter" in racial matters. Therefore,
they may behave with more hostility towards nonwhites than the
more secure members of the system do.

HYPOTHESIS TWO

Members of groups discriminated against, no matter what their
position on the lower part of the structural ladder, will manifest
similar psychological traits, particularly self-doubt, self-hate, and

negative self-concept. Most nonwhite groups have attempted, at least for a time, to escape these effects through such common techniques as name-changes and hair-straightening. Certain life-styles usually attributable to lower social classes (inability to take financial risks, a fate orientation, conformity, and distrust of politicians) are probably also related to nonwhite status. Essentially, being nonwhite means a hatred of one's own background, one's home, one's parents, and one's family.

Two black psychiatrists, Grier and Cobbs,[8] illustrate the relationship between being black in our society and psychological damage. The methodological dehumanization process reaches its peak in the exploitation and the treatment of the Negro. Feelings of rage go essentially unnoticed and the unwillingness of white Americans to accept Negroes as fellow human beings may eventually result in a violent explosion. The psychological process of self-hate, and self-denigration is related to the discrepancy between expectations and opportunities. Grier and Cobbs describe the following:

> A group of relatively poor black mothers who were seen in therapy appeared at first glance to be in their forties or fifties. They were, however, all in their late twenties. Their shapeless garments, unattractive shoes, dental neglect, and general disinterest in their appearance made them seem twenty to thirty years older than they actually were.

Because of the impossibility of ever becoming white (and therefore beautiful or attractive), these women had given up the struggle of femininity and diverted their interests elsewhere. The authors also cite the higher incidence of obesity among black women as another symptom of this struggle.

As Grier and Cobbs emphasize, a sick white man can alter his environment by escaping harmful relationships, the black man cannot. Those pressures which made the black man sick pervade all of America—the irony is that for *all nonwhites* the logical means of escape are essentially closed. For example, some may think of going back to Japan, or to China, or to Mexico, or to Africa—most will discover that they are "too American" for the mother country and therefore marginal over there, and marginal in America for being too ethnic. And the final irony is uncovered when, returning to the

---

[8] William Grier and Price Cobbs, *Black Rage* (New York: Basic Books Inc., Publishers, 1968), pp. 47–48.

mother country, the visitor finds himself defending America, including its racism, to skeptical overseas audiences.

Those groups closer to acceptability often face a more subtle struggle. Name changes, minor operations and other efforts to remove the stigmata may be attempted. And there will be those individuals within the nonwhite structures who fit more closely the negative stereotypes and bear the brunt of in-group hostility. The Japanese with buck teeth and weak eyes; the Chinese with a strong accent; the darker, more Indian-looking Mexican, and the dark Negro with big feet share the common fate of reminding their peers of the stigma of race and inferiority.

What happens to minorities in their desire to become more like the whites is best illustrated in ordinary conversation. A usual question for the Japanese is, "Is he tall?" Or for the Negro, "Is he light?" For the expectation of tall white for groups who are short or dark provides one measure of the built-in alienation of nonwhite groups in a two-category stratification system.

But the effects on self are mediated by the culture of the ethnic group. Some groups are cohesive, with the strength of history and of structures such as a strong family system, while others are virtually defenseless against the hostile assaults. Therefore, a sub-hypothesis is that *psychological variations by the target group are related to their culture*. By culture we refer to their structures and institutions, their values, expectations, and goals. Strong cultures may attain a greater cohesion during periods of stress while weaker ones may further disintegrate under such conditions. Other variables which have been shown to affect adaptation include size, geographical location, color, and nationality.

Generally, the most successful nonwhite groups are those whose cultures are most compatible with WASP values. The Japanese [9] are the closest, with high emphasis on education, hard work, saving, and delayed gratification. For a time they were considered the most dangerous because of their "pushiness," of "wanting what white Americans wanted," but over the long haul, the congruence between the American and Japanese cultures has led to a successful amalgamation. Similarly, the Chinese, with a strongly pluralistic system, have been relatively successful in America. We mean suc-

[9] Harry H. L. Kitano, *Japanese Americans: The Evolution of a Subculture* (Englewood Cliffs, N.J.: Prentice-Hall, Inc., 1969).

cessful in the sense of adapting to the WASP culture with a minimum of conflict.

Subcultures shape the means of "attacking" the enemy. For example, a series of articles in the *San Francisco Chronicle* [10] underscore some subcultural differences. In attempting to cope with window smashing and demonstrations in San Francisco's Chinatown, a Chinese spokesman warned that the phenomenon of black and yellow rebellion is different and that it would be an error to apply the Kerner report to the Chinese. He was talking about the objects of attack. For the Negro, violence is directed against the "outsiders" and the "whites," but for the Chinese youth, it is directed against the "insiders," specifically the Chinese elders of his community.

When the Japanese were placed in evacuation camps, their aggression was directed primarily against each other. [11] Fights between generations were common, and so were conflicts between those who were considered pro- and anti-American. Psychiatric evidence [12] also indicates a high amount of internalization and somatization among the Japanese so that one common reaction to frustration and stress is through internal body disorders such as stomach trouble, rather than the "acting out" through violent behavior which is more typically American.

Previous Mexican strategies called for "passing" through name changes or by identifying oneself as Spanish rather than Mexican. And of course for all groups, there are those who take advantage of their ethnicity for exploitive purposes.

However, strategies and enemies change over time. The common nonwhite reaction of self-hate, of attempting to change one's own identity to correspond more closely with the "All-American Image" is now in the historical past. To hate self, to hate family, to hate parents, to hate community, to hate nationality, and to hate one's own ethnicity is a heavy psychological burden. *All* nonwhite groups are going through the process of re-awakening and reassessing their identities which is a healthy process, although its short-term effects may lead to more conflict. To be black is now

[10] *San Francisco Chronicle*, August 19, 20, and 21, 1968.
[11] H. L. Kitano, *op. cit.*
[12] H. L. Kitano, "Japanese-American Mental Illness," in *Determinants of Mental Illness*, S. Plog and R. Edgerton, eds. (New York: Holt, Rinehart & Winston, Inc.) in press.

beautiful—similarly, to be brown or to be yellow are no longer characteristics considered as stigmas.

HYPOTHESIS THREE

The third hypothesis describes the effects of the two-category system on the white or superior group. In essence, it states that because of the stratification system, feelings of superiority are engendered among the whites and as a result there is a strong emotion to retain the boundaries. Instead of perceiving the boundary as an artificial attempt to retain the dichotomy between races, the majority group member will tend to view the split between races as one of a superior to inferior way of life, so that a prime justification for separation relates to standards. Those positioned in the upper half can then view boundary maintenance in role-prescriptive terms— if they, meaning the nonwhites, would conform to "our values," "our standards," and "our way of life," then the problem will be solved.

There are corresponding predictable psychological outcomes. For many, there arises a feeling of superiority, of a noblesse oblige, of a paternalism towards people in the nonwhite category. For others, there may be outright hate, hostility, and a repugnance against "those animals." For some there may be feelings of shame and guilt, and for the majority there will be the ability to ignore the problem, or to assume that no major racial issue exists until something as dramatic as a riot is brought to their attention.

Strain is introduced into the system because categories (e.g., nonwhite) are stressed rather than personal judgment. The rigidity of the judgment (e.g., all whites are superior to nonwhites) often leads to rationalizations, repressions, and denials. Sometimes the use of exceptions reduces strain, such as the phrase, "Of course, he's an unusual Negro."

A dangerous moment in race relations occurs when there is a call for racial solidarity against a group. Then individual sentiments and judgments are buried under cries for group cohesion—"Jap lover," "nigger lover" and other epithets are difficult to fight against, especially when one is running for political office. The same dynamic, of course, holds true for groups in the opposing camp. It is probable that those most active in maintaining the boundaries are able to switch targets without major difficulty.

Under conditions calling for racial cohesion and solidarity, the racial liberal runs the risk of being viewed as a traitor. White groups that "don't act white" also become the targets of bitter attacks—communists, hippies—and terms used to describe the "traitors" are as pejorative as racial epithets, sometimes even more so.

There is one other important point relating to racism. It is popular to assume that there is a constant liberal position, so that the social welfare, economic, and political liberal, will also be liberal on racial matters. Our evidence throws doubt on this assumption—liberals such as Supreme Court Justices Warren and Douglas were in favor of the Japanese evacuation, and labor unions (often classified as liberal) were among the foremost agitators for California racism. Many of our Southern congressmen also exhibit similar behavior. The dimension of race appears to be primarily independent of other ideological positions.

HYPOTHESIS FOUR

There is a relationship between the variables leading to permeability and the search for revolutionary changes in the racial stratification system. Those groups who find the boundaries most rigid will eventually search for different ways of resolving the discrepancy between expectations and opportunities. This hypothesis is similar to the means-ends theories of Merton, Cloward, and Ohlin, which attempt to explain deviant behavior in terms of a disjunction between expectations and the absence of legitimate opportunities. Under such conditions, feelings of alienation and anomie may develop, and search for need satisfaction through the development and use of alternate opportunity structures, including those labeled illegal or illegitimate, may follow. Revolutionary attempts at overthrowing boundaries will come from those who find permeating them most difficult.

Conversely, those groups with the highest ability to penetrate into the upper half of the two-category system will be more likely to search for within category solutions, and will usually be commended for their cooperative attitudes, and made to stand as examples of the democratic process at work. White groups wish the Negro could or would behave as the Oriental has, at the same time that their own behavior ensures that he cannot. When the Orientals were occupying the lowest position in the social structure, they did not, of course, advocate revolutionary solutions to their problems, for reasons pertaining to their subcultural structure.

Summary

In summary, although all nonwhite groups were treated similarly, reactions to their nonwhite status reflect certain subcultural variations. The Negro, the most American and the current target, is responding in a typically American fashion—through violence. The Mexican is also beginning to use tactics of organization and militancy, while the Oriental has up to now looked inwardly toward self and community.

Generally, it would be fair to say that the Japanese and Chinese were the best equipped to withstand their nonwhite status. Not only did they possess strong family and community systems and small numbers, but they were able to pass on the dream of a better life to their children. The compatibility of their values and their expectations of sharing in the American Dream place them in a position similar to other immigrant groups. The function of visibility, skin color, and racism can be inferred, however, in the relative slowness of their adaptation when compared with European immigrant groups.

Conversely, the Negro has been the least equipped to handle the hostility and disadvantage stemming from a nonwhite status. There is little question that he has been the object of the cruelest blows—the solidarity of anti-Negro prejudice and his exploitation has been consistent throughout his long stay in the United States. And with a slave heritage, broken family, and long dependence on the whites, he has been relatively helpless to combat this status in any organized manner. Interestingly enough, however, it is the Black, among all of the nonwhites, who has taken the present leadership in developing a nonwhite identity. His awakening has encouraged other nonwhite groups to question goals that were once considered inviolable, and the old criterion of success has been opened for debate. The pejorative "Uncle Tom" has found its equivalent in the Mexican "papacito" and the Japanese "Uncle Tomio." The idea of pluralism has replaced the ill-fated but perhaps not much lamented dream of the "melting pot."

6

Can It Happen Again?

One question that was raised in the beginning of this book was "Can it happen again?" We are referring to Stage 4 solutions—apartheid, expulsion, and genocide as solutions to our racial problems. We have demonstrated that these "unusual solutions" have been used before—genocide for the Indian, concentration camps for the Japanese, and various expulsion devices (if we include immigration restrictions) as a means for controlling the Oriental and Mexican populations. We present, in this chapter, a summary of the conditions which are necessary for the broaching of these final solutions.

Prior Conditions

"Ordinary solutions" to race relations provide the background conditions for extraordinary solutions. Starting with a two-category system of race relations, the strategy of the dominant group is to establish boundaries that will help maintain social distance. Therefore, prejudice, discrimination, and segregation lead to avoidance, disadvantage, and insulation—all in varying degrees of effectiveness. These conditions are prerequisite to extraordinary solutions.

Once a group is effectively isolated it can be subject to all of the stereotypes, rumors, distortions, and whatever other mechanisms appear necessary. Some of the most common faced by nonwhite groups are the following:

THE HOLLYWOOD IMAGE

Hollywood, with its mass appeal through movies and TV, has been a powerful force in maintaining stereotypes. Chinese are cooks or houseboys; Japanese are spies; Mexicans are banditos; Negroes are clowns—all of these stereotypes have appeared in countless movies. And most important, these have been the only visible images of such groups as viewed by millions of Americans.

If the nonwhite groups had intimate personal interaction with the larger culture, such distortions would have some chance for correction. But since the knowledge of these groups is often limited to what is seen on the screen, its influence is powerful. For example, children in Georgia were recently asked their opinions about Japanese. The majority who had never seen a Japanese before used the adjective "sneaky," no doubt strongly influenced by old Hollywood movies recently shown on TV about World War II.

HISTORY

Related to the Hollywood image is the consistent slighting of nonwhite groups in historical texts. Happy Negro slaves, Japanese being evacuated to concentration camps for their own protection, little mention in a positive vein of the Chinese except as coolies, emerge as general pictures of these groups. The importance of this issue is related to "feedback"—since there is no chance to correct for these sterile images, these groups remain as "nonhuman Americans," out of the mainstream.

Newspapers and other mass communications media have played active roles in racism. The names of Hearst and McClatchy are indelibly linked to early California racism.

For example, McClatchy, publisher of the influential *Sacramento Bee*, wrote in 1921:

> The Japanese cannot, may not, and will not provide desirable material for our citizenship. 1. The Japanese cannot assimilate and make good citizens because of their racial characteristics, heredity and religion. 2. The Japanese may not assimilate and make good citizens because their government claims all Japanese,

no matter where born, "as its citizens." 3. The Japanese will not assimilate and make good citizens. In the mass, when opportunity offered, and even when born here, they have shown no disposition to do so. . . . There can be no effective assimilation of Japanese without intermarriage. It is perhaps not desirable for the good of either race that there should be intermarriage between whites and Japanese. . . . They cannot be transmuted into good American citizens.[1]

Stereotypes of the nonwhites have been clear and simple, and they have been reinforced through a wide consensus among most of the mass media. Therefore, there has been a "conditioning process" by which movement towards more drastic solutions is more readily acceptable.

The conditioning process leads to a belief system that may strike an objective observer as "paranoid." For the elaborate fears of Californians concerning their relationship to nonwhites have resulted in gross distortions which are faintly amusing, except for their tragic consequences. The fixation on numbers translated into hordes, the fear of actual invasions, the denigration of groups coupled with fears of their power and superiority, the ever present sexual anxieties and the feeling that people in other states are not really acquainted with the issues, have provided fertile grounds for the move towards more drastic racial solutions.

The Normal Person

It is under the conditions of boundary maintenance, isolation and segregation that the role of the "normal person" plays such an important part in shaping towards more drastic solutions. He may not deliberately set out to destroy a group, but in the final analysis, his actions, already shaped by historical and other circumstances will be as effective as the hard core racist.

Maintaining the status quo in race relations falls back on many groups. For those with a strong commitment towards racism, there are organizations such as the White Citizens' Council and the like. We would expect a small percentage of Americans to subscribe to these extremest positions—their techniques probably appeal to the "kooks" and "lunatic fringe" and would include outright intimi-

[1] V. S. McClatchy, "Japanese in the Melting Pot: Can They Assimilate and Make Good Citizens?" in *The Annals*, Vol. XCIII, January 1921, 29–34.

dation. In the past, such behavior as lynching may have been frequent; at the present, such behavior as cross burnings, radio messages, and newsletters appear more common.

The importance of these fringe groups in race relations can probably be overemphasized. Perhaps the easiest rationalization for the normal person is to attribute *all* of the nation's racial ills to these groups—that it is the "hate-mongers" who are the primary contributors to racial tensions. These groups hold little overt power themselves—their economic resources, their use of violence, and their numbers are not that imposing when compared with the power of the normal individuals. But, their power is multiplied by a silent consensus among the vast middle group—the consensus among most whites that they are the representatives of a superior culture, and that the best solution for the nonwhites is to become more like them. And because of the barriers placed before our nonwhite groups, there is often observable evidence of white superiority.

A logical question is, "How does the normal person contribute to racial problems apart from his usual silence on most matters?" As we have indicated, the primary role of boundary maintenance falls upon certain institutions in our society. The most common are the schools, the legal and judicial system (as represented by judges, sheriffs, and the police), and the public welfare departments. The normal person wants law and order. He delegates this responsibility to these agents of "education and social control," who in the name of law and order carry out boundary maintenance tasks.

Tasks of boundary maintenance are primarily in the hands of these "normal people," with normal personalities and normal needs, holding to normal goals and normal ambitions. They work in normal jobs, make normal decisions, and are good to their families. But their positions stem from those structures most influential in maintaining the boundaries of racism.

For example, in his autobiography, Malcolm X relates how one of his most sympathetic teachers took him aside and counseled him "realistically." The message from the "nice" gatekeeper was simple —don't expect to become a lawyer, why not be a carpenter? The teacher's message for many of his less talented white cohorts was different—aim for the higher professions in life.[2]

And in the normal course of affairs, the nonwhite meets the gatekeepers and suffers. The immigration officer doing his job "catches

[2] Malcolm X and Alex Haley, *The Autobiography of Malcolm X* (New York: Grove Press, 1966), pp. 36–37.

and deports" the illegally entered Mexican and in the process ter-
rorizes an entire community; the police officer stops a "suspicious-
looking" black man and finally writes a citation for a faulty muffler;
the judge deports a Chinese immigrant who tries to obtain naturalization under a false passport; while the State attempts to escheat
the land of a Japanese alien who placed his property under the
name of his son. The particularistic and discriminatory features of
these laws which are aimed primarily at the nonwhites are seldom
questioned, and the majority of the "normals" are only dimly aware
of the disadvantaged position of the nonwhites.

Or, to take the other side of the coin—of the mob that lynched at
least twenty-two Chinamen (sic) in Los Angeles, "no serious attempt was ever made to bring the ring leaders to justice." [3] When
the Japanese were returning to the West Coast after World War II,
four whites were arrested for attacks on a Japanese farm. "The
jury acquitted all the defendants and the charge against the man
who had been arrested for illegal use of explosives was then also
dropped . . . the defendants were the center of a congratulatory
crowd after the court adjourned." [4] And the infamous "Zoot-suit
Riots" against the Mexicans in 1943 resulted in many Mexican
arrests, while no charges were brought against the white sailors who
were among the primary participants. Each nonwhite group can
no doubt add to this list of law and order without justice.

And even more drastic acts are carried out by normal, decent
men. President Roosevelt ordered the evacuation of the Japanese,
including American citizens. Colonel Bendetsen was awarded a
medal for his quick and efficient removal of the Japanese to concentration camps, and modestly replied that he was only doing his
duty. The constitutionality of the evacuation was upheld by *all*
of the Supreme Court Justices.

The problem obviously goes far beyond that of normal men
making their own individual decisions, so that a search for scape-
goats, or for those with authoritarian personalities, is not the
answer. Instead, the focus should also include the relationship
between individuals, and the structures and institutions which maintain racial separation. The Kerner Commission Report also emphasizes the institutional nature of white racism.

[3] R. G. Cleland, *A History of California, The American Period* (New York:
The Macmillan Company, 1922), p. 48.
[4] A. R. Fisher, *Exile of a Race* (Seattle, Wash.: F&T Publishers, 1965),
p. 196.

COULD THERE HAVE BEEN GENOCIDE?

It is difficult to reconstruct the events of the wartime evacuation without asking the question, could there have been a mass extermination of the Japanese, such as that of the Jews in Germany? Obviously any answer will be speculative, but we hypothesize that it would be difficult to remain optimistic if the following events had occurred:

1. What if the Japanese continued to win the war and actually invaded the Pacific Coast?
2. What if there were executions of American civilians—or mass bombardment of American cities with a high loss of American civilian lives?
3. What if the Japanese Americans actively revolted in the concentration camps? The camp at Tule Lake was a very rebellious one and control there was much more stringent.
4. What if Japan had developed a nuclear weapon and totally destroyed an American city?

The purpose of asking these questions, of course, is to emphasize that the extermination of a minority is not totally out of the realm of probability, especially when the group is already in an extremely vulnerable position, and consensus is against them. It would also be an error to discount the mood of the times. For example, a survey by Bloom and Riemer in 1943 showed that 63 percent of college students on the West Coast and 73 percent attending Midwestern schools felt that the evacuation of the Japanese was correct.[5] And there will always be enough individuals occupying strategic role positions who will follow orders and "do their duty" so that once momentum is established towards a final solution, the actions are difficult to stop.

The Mechanisms

Extraordinary solutions require major triggering mechanisms. Those "milder" mechanisms of boundary maintenance, if one considers laws and physical intimidation as mild, have been tried and found wanting. Therefore, more drastic solutions are required. The trigger includes events external to the target group

[5] L. Bloom and R. Riemer, "Attitudes of College Students Towards Japanese-Americans," *Sociometry*, 8, No. 2, May 1945.

and those actions arising primarily from within the target group. The one common element of both events is the "waiving of constitutional guarantees"—either because of the external trigger—a declaration of war—or the occurrence of internal events—the group breaks the "law."

The wartime evacuation of the Japanese provides an example between an external trigger and the approach towards a final solution. As we have described, "ordinary solutions" were tried against the Japanese and were deemed to have failed. In spite of harassment at all levels, there were still Japanese in California and they were begetting American-born citizen children. Therefore, the outbreak of World War II provided the trigger for their mass evacuation.

The Watts riot of August 1965, provides an example of an "internal trigger." Ordinary solutions to the Negro problem had failed. The residents of Watts themselves challenged the two-category system, and in the ensuing debacle blacks were killed, their area was sealed off, and many basic freedoms were denied them until there was a cessation of hostilities. This incident was much more severe than a Stage 3 solution and approached a Stage 4 apartheid situation. In fact, many blacks underline the similarity between their present situation and apartheid—they ask the rhetorical question, "Have you been black and 'out of your area' at night?"

Other conditions are associated with extraordinary solutions. The majority group perceives a danger to their very existence ("our very way of life is at stake"); the target group takes on nonhuman qualities (dogs, pigs, animals); there is a crystallization of feelings (traitor, enemy), and the perceived retaliatory power of the target group must be low. The most severe punishment (e.g., extermination) is usually reserved for a target group perceived as a nonhuman enemy, whose alien ways, if allowed, might threaten the very foundations of the society. Further, the perceived retaliatory power of the group (including their local and international alliances) must be low. This description fits that of the American Indian against whom the grossest massacres have taken place.

Unplanned Obsolescence

The role of the nonwhites in our society falls under a concept we term unplanned obsolescence. Most were imported for their labor, and if any group, including their progeny, had been content to remain permanent laborers, then the need for more than one nonwhite group may have been eliminated in California. But the beauty of the American Dream is that it stretched over *all groups*, including the nonwhites, so that in spite of the artificial boundaries of the two-category system, American expectations were incorporated as a goal by all. Therefore, as groups "served their time" in the basement, they moved up the ladder, to be replaced by other pariahs. The peculiar needs of California agriculture heightened the process. Therefore, the target groups changed—pejoratives and ways of thinking about them quickly became obsolete and new groups filled the vacuum. But since there is a basic incongruence among American democracy, American expectations, and the two-category racial system in which nonwhite groups can rise only up to a limited point, there comes a time when an honest appraisal of what has happened becomes necessary. Symptoms of discontent and of the malfunctioning of the system eventually become obvious, even to the most myopic observer.

We believe that now is the time for such an appraisal. Current data show the disadvantaged position of the nonwhite groups in relation to the whites.[6] Even the most highly educated group, the Japanese in California, make less than the less educated white group. Nonwhites are consistently relegated to the ghettoes or near ghettoes, they are still most vulnerable to depressions and unemployment, and their physical features still bring forth adverse reactions from the white majority.

But this peculiar state cannot continue forever—inevitably groups denied the opportunities of becoming "American" in the full sense of the word will react. Previous reactions to the extent of becoming 110 percent American will not suffice today, because for nonwhites to become white Anglo-Saxon Protestants is now viewed as impossible. Even the desirability of this goal is now under question—what is so magical about becoming like the white middle-class?

There are signs of a budding unity among populations in the lower half of the two-category system. All of California's nonwhite groups are sharing in this process and there is some indication that

---

[6] See United States Census of Population, 1960, Nonwhite Population by Race, U.S. Department of Commerce, Bureau of the Census and two publications of the Division of Fair Employment Practices, State of California, titled *Californians of Spanish Surname* (May 1964) and *Californians of Japanese, Chinese, and Filipino Ancestry* (June 1965), San Francisco, California.

the old pattern of pitting one ethnic group against the other may no longer be a viable one. For example, Los Angeles' Oriental groups have formed a coalition called the Council of Oriental Organizations (COO) in which representatives of Chinese, Filipino, Japanese, and Korean groups discuss and plan for the solving of mutual problems. Older generations of these groups might find such a meeting impossible—past nationalistic models stand in the way of such cooperation, but younger generations are not that wedded to the past.

Their call for unity stresses the commonality of their problems and the biases of white racism. COO asks why Asians in South Vietnam are not allowed to come into the United States as refugees if displaced whites from Hungary are allowed this option. Orientals wonder about "executive-suite discrimination," which is in accordance with their present concern in upward mobility, but they also worry about the problems of the new immigrants from Asia and the problems of the less affluent Filipino communities. The common theme is one of unity of purpose so that the spectacle of Oriental groups attacking each other may be filed as past history.

The Negro and Mexican groups are also developing their identities, both as ethnic groups and as nonwhites. Blacks often use the term brother to include all nonwhites, and they receive reciprocal recognition. But the vast differences among the various subcultural groups may preclude an intimate interaction, except if white America actively tries to maintain the two-category racial system.

We hope that the signs of movement away from the two-category system are not too late. For as our developmental model indicates, the direction of the flow is an important factor, and there are indications that the stages are gradually moving towards less extraordinary solutions. Many of the old discriminatory laws have been removed, old stereotypes are being broken, and there is much more intergroup contact. Certain groups are moving up the ladder, and it is our perspective that as ethnicity fades away as an important stratification variable, social class and personality become more important ones. The "natural history model" then predicts acculturation, and eventual integration and amalgamation, and interestingly enough, once the most feared and hated group, the Japanese, appears to be following this pattern.

But the repression of two major California groups, the Mexican and the Negro, in an era of rising expectations, may follow the old adage of too little, too late. Old cliches, conveniently forgetful memories, and verbal solutions may have been appropriate in the past and may even work for a time in the present and in the future. But, the unfortunate legacy left to us by our pioneer forefathers, in the form of racism, may remain as our gravestone unless the present generation is willing to face the problems and issues with the honesty and responsibility that our generation has not employed usefully.

Conclusion:

The Ethnic Crisis of Our Time

According to Ambrose Bierce's *Devil's Dictionary*, "only God can fortell the future, but only an Historian can distort the past." Recognizing the inevitability of Bierce's definition, we hope that our distortion has been minimal. At the same time, without any claim to clairvoyance, we do think that our examination of the past does provide some clues about the shape of the future, some indication of the general direction of events.

Although contemporary observers are notoriously inaccurate in their assessment of events, it is worth noting that in the late 1960s many, if not most, of the wisest commentators on race relations in the United States saw new dangers: for many of these the greatest danger seemed to be that America was drifting or splitting into two societies. Our analysis—and our perhaps too optimistic preconceptions—leads to opposite conclusions. There have been two societies in the past. No one who thinks for even a moment about the California Indians, the Chinese, the Japanese, the Mexican Americans, and the Negroes can really believe that any of these minorities were truly integrated into our society. They were, each in their own way, separate and unequal groups, existing below and apart from the general cultural level, and only tangentially coming into contact with the majority society.

117

If this has been true throughout our past, what then is the nature of what we call the ethnic crisis of our time? That crisis consists, we think, of simply this: for the first time in our history almost all of the submerged groups in our country—groups that Gunnar Myrdal styles the "underclass"—are demanding entrance into the major institutions of our society. And, in addition, they are demanding admission on their own terms. They come often not as humble petitioners seeking boons, but as free Americans demanding what they regard as their stolen birthright. Sometimes they even ask for compound interest to cover past injustices.

It is this new militance, this rejection of the gradual Americanization process that seemed to work so well for earlier ethnic minorities—the Germans and the Irish of the mid-nineteenth century, the Italians, Greeks, Slavs, and East European Jews of the "new immigration" of the late nineteenth and early twentieth centuries—that has provoked the current crisis. And although the long range causes of the current crisis are many, the conclusion is almost inescapable that the root cause was the pervasive nature of American racism—a racism which, although it grew less and less oppressive as the twentieth century wore on, consistently refused admission into full membership in society to the vast majority of colored Americans.

We feel then that the commentators—for example the National Advisory Commission on Civil Disorders—mistake the true nature of the crisis. Since we have never had one society in this country, the danger of social mitosis does not really exist. The visible and often violent and ugly racial and ethnic clashes do not represent new fracture lines in a previously unitary society, but represent rather the friction resulting from the attempts of these groups to enter into full membership in American society. We will later attempt to assess the chances for success of this massive breakthrough attempt, but first it will be in order to note briefly the critical areas of struggle and see how the form that these struggles take differs from that waged by earlier ethnic groups.

The three areas of conflict are education, jobs, and housing, and it is clear that, by the standards of the past, significant progress is being made in each of them, particularly the first two. But it is one of the landmarks of the present crisis that gradual progress, however significant, is no longer acceptable to the militant spokesmen for minority groups, and the mere existence of these militants tends to force even the most accommodating minority spokesmen into more radical postures. The causes of this new radicalism, this ever-increasing militance, are various, but surely the following must be included among the major factors:

1. The increasing openness of American society to all white persons and to some members of nonwhite communities.
2. The "revolution of rising expectations" among nonwhites.
3. The communications revolution, particularly television, which perhaps more in its commercials than in its program content, makes clear to the poor of the ghettoes just how little they participate in our commodity-oriented society. If this is an accurate observation, it is a wonderfully ironic one. The very aspect of television so despised by radical intellectuals may well have a more profoundly revolutionary effect than a century of agitation!

Having identified the present crisis, it might be well, in the first instance, to examine some of the changes in the ethnic scene in the last quarter century. For no group have these changes been more dramatic than for the Japanese Americans. No sane observer, writing in 1942, the year of the evacuation, would have dared to predict the current high status of the group. Hailed by a leading sociologist as "our model minority," their success story can be symbolized by Senator Daniel Inouye of Hawaii, who was the keynote speaker at the Democratic National Convention in 1968. The same society that raised no significant protest when Japanese Americans were herded behind barbed wire, was willing, just twenty-six years later, to have a member of that community play a key ceremonial role within a basic political institution. The success of Senator Inouye cannot be written off as an isolated example. As previously noted, statistical examination of the socioeconomic position of both Japanese and Chinese in America shows truly remarkable achievement.

But perhaps even more symbolic of the new role of the Oriental Americans was the sudden emergence of the semanticist, S. I. Hayakawa, as a popular culture hero late in 1968. Taking over as Acting President of San Francisco State College during a period of ethnically based student unrest that had brought the school to a standstill, Hayakawa "got tough" with the protesters—largely members of the Black Students' Union—and restored at least a semblance of order with the assistance of large numbers of San Francisco police. No more popular or, at first glance unlikely, exponent of "law and order" could be imagined. Hayakawa, an authentic intellectual (one of the few real scholars to head a California state college as well as the first nonwhite to do so) nevertheless seemed to speak for the WASP middle-class. Without attempting to judge the merits of either the dispute or the disputants at San Francisco State, the alignment of the Oriental college president against the young blacks and the radical students, probably accurately reflects the direction and identification that most Oriental Americans wished to take and establish—with the middle-class white majority and against the disruptive elements beneath.

Many Mexican Americans would like to consider themselves, like many Oriental Americans, as essentially allies of the majority community and, like them, opposed to the disruptive Negro community. But the objective conditions of Mexican-American life—they are distinctly not middle class in terms of either income or education—seriously inhibit such an identification. Although an outside observer like Gunnar Myrdal sees a logical alliance between blacks and Mexican Americans—the two most numerous ethnic minorities in California—there are long-standing animosities between the two groups. Many Mexican Americans resent bitterly what they consider the favored treatment of the Negro poor and their attitudes toward Negroes are often quite similar to those of the economically disadvantaged "Anglo" community. Yet it is also apparent that there is much institutional mimesis of the black community among militant Mexican Americans. They too are pressing for community control of schools and other institutions. But, opposed to the militants, are very strong passive and conservative elements and traditions quite different from those of the blacks. There is thus a decided ambiguity within the community, although the militants seem to be gaining strength. With young and dynamic leadership—one thinks of Caesar Chavez of the Farm Workers and Julian Nava of the Los Angeles School Board—the community may be stirred to consistent mass action; however, the old passive, conservative tradition may continue to hold sway.

To imagine that either the course taken by so many Orientals—identification with the power structure and against disruptive protest—or the passivity of the Mexican Americans could in any way serve as a "model" for the Negro, is to indulge in fantasy. Equally fantastic, and much more prevalent, is what we may call the "immigrant analogy." The analogy runs something like this:

> The Germans, the Irish, the Jews, the Poles, the Orientals, etc.
> have "made it," why can't the Negroes? These groups came to
> this country poor, they were discriminated against, and look at
> them now. The Negroes want everything given to them. Negroes
> aren't willing to work for success like others have.

The fatuity of this analogy will be obvious to some, but not so obvious to many. Although it is often advanced by those who know better, many who use it do so in ignorant confidence that it is true. The defects in this false analogy are many but the essential flaw is this: the white immigrant can, in a generation or so, fairly successfully merge with the general population if he wishes. In addition, the overt tension between white and nonwhite has tended to blur differences between white ethnic groups, to "promote" all white persons.

But what of the Orientals? Certainly they are nonwhite. Has the two-category system broken down as far as Orientals are concerned? Not really. It has changed, in many ways it has weakened, but it still remains essentially intact. The Orientals are clearly an achieving minority and have, as a group, even surpassed the white majority in terms of educational attainment. But they remain nonwhite, and are still largely segregated in terms of housing, social life, and of course, marriage. Even for the Oriental American—the "whitest" of the nonwhite—a total merging with the majority seems, at the very least, highly improbable in the foreseeable future, although we must here reiterate that no sane observer, writing in 1942, could have predicted the truly amazing increase in social acceptance that has occurred since then.

If this is true for the Orientals, how much more true must it be for other groups and particularly for the Negro, who is, by American criteria, the most nonwhite of all. The increasing recognition by more and more members of the black community of at least the relative permanence of the two-category system (although, of course, they do not call it that) is yet another factor contributing to the current ethnic crisis. The progress made by the Negro in the last quarter century is not as spectacular, on a mass basis, as that of the Oriental group. The educational achievement is still well below that of the general level of the population. Again, using the

1960 census data for California, Negroes are only half as likely to gain admittance to an institution of higher education as a white; Negro income is similarly depressed. Yet, for some individuals, the group that W. E. B. Du Bois once identified as the "talented tenth," there have been truly spectacular advances.

First and foremost, of course, despite the many disappointments inherent in it, was the United States Supreme Court's 9-0 decision in *Brown v. Board of Education* (1954) which outlawed segregation. Whatever failings there have been in its enforcement, and despite its almost total lack of relevance in the urban ghetto situation, it was truly a turning point. Despite local practices, it was important that federal policy, at least, was no longer *officially* racist. The Constitution had finally been brought into line with the Declaration of Independence. One should also note the ending of segregation in the armed forces and in many lines of endeavor—for example, UCLA's Jackie Robinson broke the color barrier in professional baseball, which now seems, like most sports, to be dominated by Negroes.

On the political scene the breakthrough for the Negro elite was almost equally sensational. At the end of 1968 there was a Negro, Thurgood Marshall, on the Supreme Court, and another, Robert C. Weaver, in the cabinet. (Perhaps an even more telling demonstration of this breakthrough came when Richard M. Nixon announced his first cabinet—the initial reaction was that there was not a Negro in it, although only the preceding cabinet had had a Negro.) Impressive electoral victories were scored, North and South. Most impressive, perhaps, was Edward Brooke's capture of a U.S. Senate seat in Massachusetts, specifically because he had no statistically significant Negro vote base, as did almost all the other Negroes who had ever been elected. Of more consequence was the election of Negro mayors in Cleveland, Ohio and Gary, Indiana, and the 385 state and local Negro office holders in the South. In California the contingent of Negro office holders—the first had been state assemblyman Frederic M. Roberts elected from Los Angeles in 1918!—grew with every election. Augustus Hawkins of Los Angeles was one of the state's senior congressmen and state legislators like Willie Brown of San Francisco and Mervyn Dymally of Los Angeles were important figures. In Los Angeles there were three Negro city councilmen, slightly more than the numerical incidence of Negroes in the city population would indicate. In terms of local elective office, in California at least, it can be argued that Negroes have achieved almost their "fair" share of representation. But the illusory nature of that "fairness" was spelled out in no uncertain terms in the Los Angeles mayoralty elections in the spring of 1969.

In the April primary Thomas R. Bradley, one of the city's three black councilmen, led all candidates with some 42 percent of the vote. Since Negroes make up less than 20 percent of the electorate, Bradley had won more white votes than black. The incumbent mayor, Samuel W. Yorty, polled only 26 percent of the vote. By the normal rules of California politics an incumbent rejected by almost three-quarters of the electorate has almost no chance in the runoff, but any election that pits black against white is not normal. As the May 27 runoff approached, incumbent Yorty, who had run on his rather poor eight-year record in the primary, switched to a blatantly racist campaign. Bumper stickers appeared calling for "A Majority Mayor for the Majority of the People" and Yorty himself constantly spoke of Los Angeles as "a city under siege by militants" and referred repeatedly to real and imaginary problems in Gary and Cleveland, cities which had elected black mayors. Although Bradley was far from being a militant and was clearly well-qualified for the office—he possessed a law degree, had been an outstanding councilman for six years and before that a police lieutenant with 21 years on the force—Yorty's fear campaign was successful. In the runoff election he received some 53 percent of the vote to Bradley's 46 percent. The election demonstrated clearly the racist nature of the electorate. Despite disillusionment with Yorty, the real choice of only a quarter of the voters, a majority was willing to continue him (or probably any white man) in office rather than try a black man. Although it is possible to emphasize the positive aspects of Bradley's performance—after all most of his votes did not come from the black community—the election could only serve to heighten the already prevalent mood of disenchantment in the Negro community.

Disenchantment was derived from that part of the American Dream which emphasized total integration. Black Americans were vocally denying that the melting pot—that archtypical American myth—would ever merge black and white. Actually, as ethnic historians like Will Herberg pointed out some time ago, there has been no real melting pot, even for whites. Herberg called attention to what he called a "triple melting pot" in which Catholics, Protestants, and Jews, largely maintained their own identities but tended, after a couple of generations, to pay less attention to ethnic differences within the religion. If the melting pot has actually dissolved so few of the differences between whites, was it reasonable to expect it to blend black into white? Most Negro leaders today, and particularly those of the younger generation, would give a resounding "No" to that question, and we, however reluctantly, are forced to conclude that they are right. The two-category system, in some form or other, is likely to be with us for some time. Negroes, Mexican Americans, and Orientals are probably going to continue to exist as at least partially self-contained and self-conscious communities within our society for generations. Social scientists and others, then, would probably do well to concentrate their efforts on making the two-category system work as well as possible.

When we say this we are neither advocating nor predicting an American version of apartheid, although that remains a distinct, if somewhat remote, possibility. We are not endorsing this as an optimum social system. What we are saying is that our observation and analysis of American ethnic history and practice lead unambiguously to this conclusion.

This being the case, our analysis of certain trends in the black community—a trend toward black nationalism, ethnic pride and, in extreme cases, a black separatism and black racism that is a curious mirror image of white racism—leads us to argue that they are almost inevitable, and that these trends are, in their major emphasis, a manifestation of a keener awareness of social reality than is shown by the more socially acceptable positions of such organizations as the National Association for the Advancement of Colored People. In saying this we are not endorsing such chimeras as an independent Negro republic carved out of U.S. territory, or, on the academic level, some of the more extreme demands of the various Black Student Unions. One author (Daniels) recently participated in an angry meeting with a B.S.U. spokesman who vainly tried to convince a faculty committee that only blacks should teach and lecture on subjects concerning blacks. This kind of racism is neither rational nor viable, but in condemning and rejecting it we should remember that, historically speaking, there is a distinct difference between the origins of white and black racism. The first is an instrument of oppression; the second a response to oppression.

But short of the extreme position—and the electoral performance of Negroes in the 1968 elections suggests that more than 90 percent of voting Negro Americans are well short of it—there remains a decided trend among blacks, in and out of the ghetto, towards community control of those things which most directly affect the community: schools, jobs, and housing.

In no area is the selective nature of black nationalism more clearly demonstrated than in education. In terms of the public school system, kindergarten through high school, black communities throughout the nation are struggling, with various degrees of success, to gain control of the schools in their areas. The tactics will vary from school district to school district depending on the militancy of the blacks and the degree of intransigence of the groups that usually oppose them: the school boards, the teachers and the white community. But from New York to Los Angeles the basic tenor of the demands is essentially the same. Throughout the nation the schools that the majority of urban Negroes attend are all black or predominantly black because they are located in all black or predominantly black neighborhoods. The years since the Supreme Court's decision in 1954 have actually witnessed an intensification of this de facto segregation. As a general rule these segregated schools—for a variety of reasons, not all of them explicitly racist—are distinctly inferior in physical plant, equipment, and in teaching personnel.

Black communities, from coast to coast, are tending to give up the struggle for ethnic balance in the schools and are instead beginning to accept what seems to them the inevitable and at least semi-permanent fact of de facto segregation. Their new demands focus on black control of schools for blacks—black school boards, black principals, more black teachers, and a curriculum more oriented to the realities of ghetto life. This struggle, just beginning, has already involved violence, an interruption of the educational process, and the alienation of some of the white liberal support which the black community has enjoyed in recent years.

On the college and university level, however, the same struggle has taken an entirely different form. Although there have been isolated demands for more Negro colleges and universities in the North, the real thrust of the new militance at the college level has been for the recognition of a black identity within the existing college and university structure. The typical instruments for these demands are the Black Student Unions, almost always self-segregating organizations with alliances connecting them to radical student groups, with the latter becoming more and more white in the process. The typical demands of the BSUs and their allies are for more black students, black professors, and a black or Afro-American studies area within the curriculum. Of these demands, the second seems the hardest to satisfy, simply because, as in other "trade union" situations, few Negroes have the requisite union card, in this case the doctoral degree. The university community is adjusting to these demands with varying degrees of success. Several California universities have set up at least rudimentary courses and programs in black history and culture. In late 1968, in a move almost sure to be emulated elsewhere, Yale University lent its enormous prestige to one aspect of BSU demands by announcing the establishment of an interdisciplinary major in Afro-American studies.

More than any other institution in American society, the higher educational establishment has shown itself willing to adapt at least partially to the new black demands. Crucial to this goal have been a variety of public and private programs aimed at upgrading the educational opportunities for the poor in general, and the disadvantaged ethnic poor in particular. These programs, like the federally financed Head Start for pre-schoolers, Upward Bound for high school students, and such private activities as the Danforth Foundation's Masters Opportunity Program which subsidizes Negro and Mexican-American college graduates in search of an M.A., are all initial steps toward eradicating the educational disadvantage of the ethnic poor which is one of the hallmarks of American racism. These programs so far have involved only a very minor fraction of those who need them and if they are to be more than another token movement, their scope and funding will have to be increased enormously.

In terms of jobs, the same kind of selective black nationalism has asserted itself. There is a growing emphasis on black entrepreneurship in the ghettoes. While no one should underestimate the importance of developing a stronger black entrepreneurial class or what is sometimes called "black capitalism," the basic facts of American economic life severely inhibit the role that can be played by small businessmen, regardless of their color or ethnicity. The business of America, to paraphrase Calvin Coolidge, is corporate business, and the trend toward giantism, toward the conglomerate super corporation is growing more pronounced every year. A major part of the new economic thrust of the blacks, therefore, has been a concentrated attack on the barriers erected by the white-controlled power structures: the corporations and the trade unions. Their weapons have been the anti-discrimination edicts of various branches of government, largely the federal government, and to a lesser degree, economic boycotts (and sometimes physical destruction) of the ghetto branches of white corporations—supermarkets, service stations, and the like.

There is obviously an increased willingness on the part of corporations to hire *qualified* members of disadvantaged ethnic communities at all levels, and, in some cases, to lower or alter certain of their requirements, like the intelligence tests for factory workers, which, by accident or design, are oriented to favor those with a majority cultural background. By the late 1960s, corporate recruiters were actually seeking more Negro college graduates than they could find. Some corporations were beginning to locate plants in or adjacent to the ghettoes. Even in television commercials—not exactly the most enlightened area of American culture—the Negro consumer has suddenly become visible, although there are still such probably unintentional slurs as advertisements for flesh-colored bandages. For the educated ethnic minority, decent jobs are no longer a problem, although the matter of promotion, particularly to positions in which a minority group member could hire and fire whites, is often something else again. On the other hand, according to the *Wall Street Journal*, Negro engineering graduates in 1968 got higher starting salaries than did whites. This was the result of federal insistence that firms with government contracts, particularly defense contracts, show evidence of nondiscriminatory employment at all levels, coupled with a very small crop of Negro engineers. (Demand exceeded supply, so the price went up.)

But for vast numbers of the ethnic unemployed—the drop-outs, the functional illiterates, the unskilled—little real possibility of private employment exists. In an earlier era our industrial labor force could absorb—in good times—almost unlimited numbers of immigrants who often had nothing but brawn to offer. Today our increasingly sophisticated economy needs less "muscle" every year. Thus there are literally millions of healthy Americans for whom no real economic opportunity exists, regardless of their willingness to work. The much heralded training and retraining programs—public and private—have reached an even smaller portion of their potential constituency than have the programs for the educationally disadvantaged. This problem, too, has its roots in the cultural deprivation of past American racist policy. The programs and phenomena described in the preceding sentences will at least inhibit the production of future generations of "unemployables," but even if every youngster of school age in America's ethnic ghettoes were assured of an education adequate for today's complex society (a state of affairs not likely to come about soon) unemployables of adult years would be with us for decades. The fact of the matter is that the number, if not the percentage, of such persons is growing with every passing year. There will be no real peace in the ghettoes until every able-bodied person who wants to work is furnished with a job or meaningful access to a training program that will provide him with the means of getting one.

In the field of housing there has been less progress than in the areas of education and employment, partially because no significant sector of the economy is so "privatized," so atomistic, so archaic. Despite a number of government housing programs, dating back to the New Deal, there is in the central city ghettoes more deterioration than construction every year. These central city ghettoes are growing constantly, as a result of migration from the South and Puerto Rico. The militants of the black communities are much more interested now in controlling the ghetto communities and making them better places in which to live than in trying to "break out" into white or partially integrated suburbs. Apart from desire, most ghetto residents lack the means to move. We may assume then, that the ghetto is here to stay. It is also safe to assume that as part of their attempt to gain more control over their own lives, blacks and other ghetto residents will move increasingly towards community organizations, organizations that will stress self-help and attempt to attract public and private financial and technical assistance. In Los Angeles, the Watts' Labor Council, headed by Ted Watkins, is perhaps a prototype of this kind of organization.

But crucial to the future of the ghettoes is the one institution of the majority society that has proved to be the least responsive to the plight of the ethnically disadvantaged—the police. No major institution of American life is less amenable to outside control, more contemptuous of "civilian" criticism. No institution of the majority society is more resented by the ghetto dweller. It is clear that if the black community is truly to control its own inner life, it must have some control or influence over the forces that police it. As yet this goal has not been achieved anywhere. Even the election of a Negro mayor in Cleveland has not noticeably lessened—and may possibly have intensified—tensions between the black community and those whom society has deputized to preserve and protect it. The one method for outside control of the police that has been attempted— the civilian review board—has been either blocked or scuttled by vigorous and astute pressure on the part of militant police groups and their allies in the white community. No one who followed the 1968 campaign can doubt the political impact of the linguistically innocuous slogan of "law and order," which became, from some rostrums, a kind of code phrase which really meant keeping the Negro in his place.

This matter of community control—of schools, of jobs, of the police, and all the other institutions which bear directly on the ghetto dweller—is likely to be the crucial issue between black and white America in the foreseeable future. It seems to us that, even within the two-category system which we find in the American past, present, and future, there are distinct possibilities for progress, for amelioration, for social peace. We suspect that this progress, if it comes at all, will come within a modified system rather than by a fracturing of the one which exists. The traditional liberal solutions and slogans—the melting pot and total integration—do not seem to us to be particularly relevant.

It is all too possible, however, that the communal clashes and conflicts which are sure to continue will harden rather than soften the mechanics of the system. It is at least within the realm of the conceivable that the cities of America will be wracked by real communal warfare. Should this occur, it would undoubtedly be accompanied by an intensification of the so-called white backlash in the majority community. It would be foolish to attempt to predict in detail the forms that oppression might take in such an eventuality, but certainly the concentration camps provided for in the McCarran Act of 1950 are a distinct possibility.

It is not likely, however, that a total or nearly total incarceration, like the wartime evacuation of the Japanese Americans, would even be seriously contemplated. On mere logistical grounds alone the size of the black community in the United States—some 25 million people—precludes that. Nor, given the American experience, is a "final solution" likely, although the charge of genocide or attempted genocide falls lightly and often from some black militant lips. One would expect, at the very least, repression, incarceration of militant groups, and perhaps a reinstitution of legal segregation with modifications designed to meet problems arising from the Northern urban environment. There would certainly be those who would look to South Africa for institutional solutions.

This gloomy prospect, we would like to emphasize, does not seem to us to represent the probable course of events. We think that, within limits, there are solutions for the ethnic crisis of our time. But societies do not always resolve their pressing problems in a rational way. A totalitarian, racist solution could happen here.

Documents

People v. Hall, 1854

Bias against Chinese and other colored "races" was endemic in Nineteenth Century California, but perhaps no single document so well demonstrates that bias as this majority opinion handed down by the Chief Justice of the California Supreme Court. Since Chinese miners lived in small, segregated groups, the practical effect of this decision was to declare "open season" on Chinese, since crimes against them were likely to be witnessed only by other Chinese.

THE PEOPLE, RESPONDENT, v. GEORGE W. HALL, APPELLANT

The appellant, a free white citizen of this State, was convicted of murder upon the testimony of Chinese witnesses.

The point involved in this case, is the admissibility of such evidence.

The 394th section of the Act Concerning Civil Cases, provides that no Indian or Negro shall be allowed to testify as a witness in any action or proceeding in which a White person is a party.

The 14th section of the Act of April 16th, 1850, regulating Criminal

131

Proceedings, provides that "No Black, or Mulatto person, or Indian, shall be allowed to give evidence in favor of, or against a white man."

The true point at which we are anxious to arrive, is the legal signification of the words, "Black, Mulatto, Indian and White person," and whether the Legislature adopted them as generic terms, or intended to limit their application to specific types of the human species.

Before considering this question, it is proper to remark the difference between the two sections of our Statute, already quoted, the latter being more broad and comprehensive in its exclusion, by use of the word "Black," instead of Negro.

Conceding, however, for the present, that the word "Black," as used in the 14th section, and "Negro," in 394th, are convertible terms, and that the former was intended to include the latter, let us proceed to inquire who are excluded from testifying as witnesses under the term "Indian."

When Columbus first landed upon the shores of this continent, in his attempt to discover a western passage to the Indies, he imagined that he had accomplished the object of his expedition, and that the Island of San Salvador was one of those Islands of the Chinese sea, lying near the extremity of India, which had been described by navigators.

Acting upon this hypothesis, and also perhaps from the similarity of features and physical conformation, he gave to the Islanders the name of Indians, which appellation was universally adopted, and extended to the aboriginals of the New World, as well as of Asia.

From that time, down to a very recent period, the American Indians and the Mongolian, or Asiatic, were regarded as the same type of the human species. . . .

. . . That this was the common opinion in the early history of American legislation, cannot be disputed, and, therefore, all legislation upon the subject must have borne relation to that opinion. . . .

. . . In using the words, "No Black, or Mulatto person, or Indian shall be allowed to give evidence for or against a White person," the Legislature, if any intention can be ascribed to it, adopted the most comprehensive terms to embrace every known class or shade of color, as the apparent design was to protect the White person from the influence of all testimony other than that of persons of the same caste. The use of these terms must, by every sound rule of construction, exclude every one who is not of white blood. . . .

. . . We have carefully considered all the consequences resulting from a different rule of construction, and are satisfied that even in a doubtful case we would be impelled to this decision on grounds of public policy.

The same rule which would admit them to testify, would admit them to all the equal rights of citizenship, and we might soon see them at the polls, in the jury box, upon the bench, and in our legislative halls.

This is not a speculation which exists in the excited and overheated imagination of the patriot and statesman, but it is an actual and present danger.

The anomalous spectacle of a distinct people, living in our community, recognizing no laws of this State except through necessity, bringing with them their prejudices and national feuds, in which they indulge in open violation of law; whose mendacity is proverbial; a race of people whom nature has marked as inferior, and who are incapable of progress or intellectual development beyond a certain point, as their history has shown; differing in language, opinions, color, and physical conformation; between whom and ourselves nature has placed an impassable difference, is now presented, and for them is claimed, not only the right to swear away the life of a citizen, but the further privilege of participating with us in administering the affairs of our Government. . . .

. . . For these reasons, we are of opinion that the testimony was inadmissible. . . .

California Constitution, 1876

In 1876, at the height of the anti-Chinese movement, California adopted a new constitution. Its anti-Chinese provisions, largely unenforceable, represent an accurate measure of public feeling.

ARTICLE XIX

Section 1. The Legislature shall prescribe all necessary regulations for the protection of the State, and the counties, cities, and towns thereof, from the burdens and evils arising from the presence of aliens, who are or may become vagrants, paupers, mendicants, criminals, or invalids afflicted with contagious or infectious diseases, and from aliens otherwise dangerous or detrimental to the well-being or peace of the State, and to impose conditions upon which such persons may reside in the State, and to provide means and mode of their removal from the State upon failure or refusal to comply with such conditions; provided, that nothing contained in this section shall be construed to impair or limit the power of the Legislature to pass such police laws or other regulations as it may deem necessary.

Section 2. No corporation now existing or hereafter formed under the laws of this State, shall, after the adoption of this Constitution, employ, directly or indirectly, in any capacity, any Chinese or Mongolian. The Legislature shall pass such laws as may be necessary to enforce this provision.

Section 3. No Chinese shall be employed on any State, county, municipal, or other public work, except in punishment for crime.

Section 4. The presence of foreigners ineligible to become citizens of the United States is declared to be dangerous to the well-being of the State, and the Legislature shall discourage their immigration by all the means within its power. Asiatic coolieism is a form of human slavery, and is forever prohibited in this State; and all contracts for coolie labor shall be void. All companies or corporations, whether formed in this country or any foreign country, for the importation of such labor, shall be subject to such penalties as the Legislature may prescribe. The Legislature shall delegate all necessary power to the incorporated cities and towns of this State for the removal of Chinese without the limits of such cities and towns, or for their location within prescribed portions of those limits; and it shall also provide the necessary legislation to prohibit the introduction into this State of Chinese after the adoption of this Constitution. This section shall be enforced by appropriate legislation.

The Relocation of the
Japanese Americans, 1942

This Executive Order, although it does not mention Japanese Americans by name, was the legal authority by which 112,000 people were forced to leave their homes and were sent to "Relocation Camps" in the interior of the United States. Congress quickly gave its sanction with appropriate legislation.

EXECUTIVE ORDER: AUTHORIZING THE SECRETARY OF WAR TO PRESCRIBE MILITARY AREAS

WHEREAS the successful prosecution of the war requires every possible protection against espionage and against sabotage to national-defense material, national-defense premises, and national-defense utilities as defined in Section 4, Act of April 20, 1918, 40 Stat. 533, as amended by the Act of November 30, 1940, 54 Stat. 1220, and the Act of August 21, 1941, 55 Stat. 655 (U.S.C., Title 50, Sec. 104):

NOW, THEREFORE, by virtue of the authority vested in me as President of the United States, and Commander in Chief of the Army and Navy, I hereby authorize and direct the Secretary of War, and the Military Commanders whom he may from time to time designate, whenever he or any designated Commander deems such action necessary or desirable, to prescribe military areas in such places and of such extent as he or the appropriate Military Commander may determine, from which any or all persons may be excluded, and with respect to which, the right of any person to enter, remain in, or leave shall be subject to whatever restrictions the Secretary of War or the appropriate Military Commander may impose in his discretion. The Secretary of War is hereby authorized to provide for residents of any such area who are excluded therefrom, such transportation, food, shelter, and other accommodations as may be necessary, in the judgment of the Secretary of War or the said Military Commander, and until other arrangements are made, to accomplish the purpose of this order. The designation of military areas in any region or locality shall supersede designations of prohibited and restricted areas by the Attorney General under the Proclamations of December 7 and 8, 1941, and shall supersede the responsibility and authority of the Attorney General under the said Proclamations in respect of such prohibited and restricted areas.

I hereby further authorize and direct the Secretary of War and the said Military Commanders to take such other steps as he or the appropriate Military Commander may deem advisable to enforce compliance with the restrictions applicable to each Military area hereinabove authorized to be designated, including the use of Federal troops and other Federal Agencies, with authority to accept assistance of state and local agencies.

I hereby further authorize and direct all Executive Departments, independent establishments and other Federal Agencies, to assist the Secretary of War or the said Military Commanders in carrying out this Executive Order, including the furnishing of medical aid, hospitalization, food, clothing, transportation, use of land, shelter, and other supplies, equipment, utilities, facilities, and services.

This order shall not be construed as modifying or limiting in any way the authority heretofore granted under Executive Order No. 8972, dated December 12, 1941, nor shall it be construed as limiting or modifying the duty and responsibility of the Federal Bureau of Investigation, with respect to the investigation of alleged acts of sabotage or the duty and responsibility of the Attorney General and the Department of Justice under the Proclamations of December 7 and 8, 1941, prescribing regulations for the conduct and control of alien enemies, except as such duty and responsibility is superseded by the designation of military areas hereunder.

The White House,   FRANKLIN D. ROOSEVELT
February 19, 1942
[No. 9066]

Ethnic Educational and Economic Achievement, California—1960

Nothing shows the social disadvantagement of ethnic groups quite so clearly as education and income data. Note that for certain groups, despite high educational achievement, income remains depressed and that the "white" figures are depressed by the Spanish surname data. The tables were compiled by the Division of Fair Employment Practices, State of California, and appear in their publication CALIFORNIANS OF JAPANESE, CHINESE, AND FILIPINO ANCESTRY *(San Francisco, 1965).*

Educational attainment	Percent of population 14 years old and over	
	Male	Female
Not having gone beyond 8th grade		
Filipino	53.1	30.6
Spanish surname	51.5	48.0
Chinese	40.8	38.7
Negro	37.9	34.0
White (including Spanish surname)	27.2	24.4
Japanese	19.5	20.1
Having completed one or more years of high school		
Filipino	46.9	69.4
Spanish surname	48.5	52.0
Chinese	59.2	61.3
Negro	62.1	66.0
White (including Spanish surname)	72.8	75.6
Japanese	80.5	79.9
Having completed one or more years of college		
Spanish surname	8.8	6.2
Negro	12.7	13.6
Filipino	13.4	24.3
White (including Spanish surname)	24.1	19.6
Japanese	28.8	20.6
Chinese	29.2	23.2

Population group	Median annual income in 1959, persons 14 years of age and over, California	
	Male	Female
Filipino	$2,925	$1,591
Negro	3,553	1,596
Chinese	3,803	1,997
Spanish surname	3,849	1,534
Japanese	4,388	2,144
White (including Spanish surname)	5,109	1,812

ANNUAL INCOME OF MEN 25 YEARS OLD
AND OVER, CALIFORNIA, 1959

Population group	Under $2,000	Under $3,000	Under $5,000
Filipino	27.6 percent	48.0 percent	79.2 percent
Negro	22.0 percent	34.2 percent	70.9 percent
Chinese	21.2 percent	33.6 percent	61.6 percent
Spanish surname	20.8 percent	30.9 percent	59.9 percent
Japanese	16.5 percent	26.1 percent	52.9 percent
White (including Spanish surname)	14.1 percent	21.1 percent	40.4 percent

Commission on the Los Angeles Riots—1965

This report on the Watts riots of August 1965, was prepared by a commission headed by John J. McCone, former head of the Central Intelligence Agency. Much criticized by liberals and activists, it was the first major public document to recognize that compensatory treatment rather than pro forma equality was necessary in many areas. Most of the recommendations were not put into effect.

RECOMMENDATIONS

LAW ENFORCEMENT

1) The Board of Police Commissioners should be strengthened.

2) Investigations of all citizen complaints should be conducted by an independent Inspector General under the authority of the Chief of Police in the implementation of procedures established by the Board of Police Commissioners.

3) The Police Department should institute expanded community relations programs.

4) The Sheriff's Department should effectuate these recommendations to the extent that they are applicable to it.

EMPLOYMENT

1) There should immediately be developed in the affected area a job training and placement center through the combined efforts of Negroes, employers, labor unions, and government.

2) Federal and state governments should seek to insure, through the development of new facilities and additional means of communication, that maximum advantage is taken of government and private training programs and employment opportunities in our disadvantaged communities.

3) Legislation should be enacted requiring employers with more than 250 employees and all labor unions to report annually to the State Fair Employment Practices Commission the racial composition of their work force and membership.

EDUCATION

1) Elementary and junior high schools in the disadvantaged areas which have achievement levels substantially below the city average should be designated as "Emergency Schools." In

each of these schools, an "Emergency Literacy Program" should be established consisting of a drastic reduction in class size to a maximum of 22 students and additional supportive personnel to provide special services. It is estimated that this program will cost at least $250 per year per student in addition to present per student costs and exclusive of capital expenditures, and that it must be continued for a minimum of six years for the elementary schools and three years for the junior high schools.

2) A permanent pre-school program should be established throughout the school year to provide education beginning at age three. Efforts should be focused on the development of language skills essential to prepare children to learn to read and write.

SUMMARY

The study of the Los Angeles riots which we have now completed brought us face to face with the deepening problems that confront America. They are the problems of transition created by three decades of change during which the historical pattern of urban and rural life—which for decades before existed side by side, each complementing and supporting the other—has been violently and irreversibly altered. Modern methods and mechanization of the farm have dramatically, and, in some regards, sadly reduced the need for the farm hand. With this, a drift to the city was the inevitable and necessary result. With respect to the Negro, the drift was first to the urban centers of the South and then, because scanty means of livelihood existed there, on northward and westward to the larger metropolitan centers. It was not the Negro alone who drifted; a substantial part of the entire farm labor force, white and Negro alike, was forced to move and did.

World War II and, to a lesser extent, the Korean War of the early '50's, tended to accelerate the movement, particularly the drift of the Negro from the south to the north. Because job opportunities existed in the war plants located in our cities, the deep and provocative problem created by the movement was not at first appreciated by society. Since then, caught up in almost a decade of struggle with civil rights and its related problems, most of America focused its attention upon the problems of the South—and only a few turned their attention and thoughts to the explosive situation of our cities.

But the conditions of life in the urban north and west were sadly disappointing to the rural newcomer, particularly the Negro. Totally untrained, he was qualified only for jobs calling for the lesser skills and these he secured and held onto with great difficulty. Even the jobs he found in the city soon began to disappear as the mechanization of industry took over, as it has since the war, and wiped out one task after another—the only tasks the untrained Negro was equipped to fill.

Hence, equality of opportunity, a privilege he sought and expected, proved more of an illusion than a fact. The Negro found that he entered the competitive life of the city with very real handicaps: he lacked education, training, and experience, and his handicaps were aggravated by racial barriers which were more traditional than legal. He found himself, for reasons for which he had no responsibility and over which he had no control, in a situation in which providing a livelihood for himself and his family was most difficult and at times desperate. Thus, with the passage of time, altogether too often the rural Negro who has come to the city sinks into despair. And many of the younger generation, coming on in great numbers, inherit this feeling but seek release, not in apathy, but in ways which, if allowed to run unchecked, offer nothing but tragedy to America.

Realizing this, our Commission has made, in this report, many costly and extreme recommendations. We make them because we are convinced the Negro can no longer exist, as he has, with the disadvantages which separate him from the rest of society, deprive him of employment, and cause him to drift aimlessly through life.

This, we feel, represents a crisis in our country. In this report we describe the reasons and recommend remedies, such as establishment of a special school program, creation of training courses, and correction of misunderstandings involving law enforcement. Yet to do all of these things and spend the sums involved will all be for naught unless the conscience of the community, the white and the Negro community together, directs a new and, we believe, revolutionary attitude towards the problems of our city.

This demands a form of leadership that we have not found. The time for bitter recriminations is past. It must be replaced by thoughtful efforts on the part of all to solve the deepening problems that threaten the foundations of our society.

GOVERNMENT   Government authorities have done much and have been generous in their efforts to help the Negro find his place in our society and in our economy. But what has been done is but a beginning and sadly has not always reached those for whom it was intended in time and in a meaningful way. Programs must not be oversold and exaggerated, on the one hand, or unnecessarily delayed on the other. What we urge is a submersion of personal ambition either political or bureaucratic, in the interest of doing the most good and creating the best results from each and every dollar spent in existing programs.

With particular respect to the City of Los Angeles, we urge the immediate creation of a City Human Relations Commission, endowed with clear cut responsibility, properly staffed and adequately funded. We envisage a commission composed of a chairman and six members with special competence in the fields of research, employment, housing, education, law, youth problems, and community organizations. This City Commission should develop comprehensive educational programs designed to enlist the cooperation of all groups, both public and private, in eliminating prejudice and discrimination in employment, housing, education, and public accommodations.

BUSINESS AND LABOR   Business leaders have their indispensable role. No longer can the leaders of business discharge their responsibility by merely approving a broadly worded executive order establishing a policy of non-discrimination and equality of opportunity as a basic directive to their managers and personnel departments. They must insist that these policies are carried out and they must keep records to see that they are. Also, they must authorize the necessary facilities for employment and training, properly designed to encourage the employment of Negroes and Mexican-Americans, rather than follow a course which all too often appears to place almost insurmountable hurdles in the path of the Negro or Mexican-American seeking a job. Directly and through the Chamber of Commerce, the Merchants and Manufacturers Association, and other associations, the business leader can play a most important role in helping to solve the crisis in our cities.

Labor unions have their very vital role. Union leaders must be resolute in their determination to eliminate discrimination and

provide equality of opportunity for all within spheres of their juris-
diction and influence. For one reason or another, the records of the
ethnic mix of the membership of many unions have not been furnished despite our repeated requests. In labor, as in business, pro-
nouncements of policy, however well intended, are not enough.
Unless a union conducts its affairs on a basis of absolute equality
of opportunity and non-discrimination, we believe there is reason
to question its eligibility to represent employees at the bargaining
table.

NEWS MEDIA   The press, television, and radio can play their part.
Good reporting of constructive efforts in the field of race relations
will be a major service to the community. We urge all media to
report equally the good and the bad—the accomplishments of
Negroes as well as the failures; the assistance offered to Negroes by
the public and private sectors as well as the rejections.

In our study of the chronology of the riots, we gave considerable
attention to the reporting of inflammatory incidents which occurred
in the initial stage of the Los Angeles riots. It is understandably easy
to report the dramatic and ignore the constructive; yet the highest
traditions of a free press involve responsibility as well as drama. We
urge that members of all media meet and consider whether there
might be wisdom in the establishment of guide lines, completely
voluntary on their part, for reporting of such disasters. Without
restricting their essential role of carrying the news to the public
fairly and accurately, we believe news media may be able to find a
voluntary basis for exercising restraint and prudence in reporting
inflammatory incidents. This has been done successfully elsewhere.

THE NEGRO AND THE LEADER   Finally, we come to the role of the
Negro leader and his responsibility to his own people and to the
community in which he lives. The signing of the Voting Rights Act
by President Johnson in the spring of 1965 climaxed a long and bitter
fight over civil rights. To be sure, the civil rights controversy has
never been the issue in our community that it has been in the South.
However, the accusations of the leaders of the national movement
have been picked up by many local voices and have been echoed
throughout the Negro community here. As we have said in the

opening chapter of this report, the angry exhortations and the resulting disobedience to law in many parts of our nation appear to have contributed importantly to the feeling of rage which made the Los Angeles riots possible. Although the Commission received much thoughtful and constructive testimony from Negro witnesses, we also heard statements of the most extreme and emotional nature. For the most part, our study fails to support—indeed the evidence disproves —most of the statements made by the extremists. We firmly believe that progress towards ameliorating the current wrongs is difficult in an atmosphere pervaded by these extreme statements.

If the recommendations we make are to succeed, the constructive assistance of all Negro leaders is absolutely essential. No amount of money, no amount of effort, no amount of training will raise the disadvantaged Negro to the position he seeks and should have within this community—a position of equality—unless he himself shoulders a full share of the responsibility for his own well being. The efforts of the Negro leaders, and there are many able and dedicated ones among us, should be directed towards urging and exhorting their followers to this end.

The Commission recognizes that much of what it has to say about causes and remedies is not new, although it is backed up by fresh additional evidence coming out of the investigation of the Los Angeles riots. At the same time, the Commission believes that there is an urgency in solving the problems, old or new, and that all Americans, whatever their color, must become aware of this urgency. Among the many steps which should be taken to improve the present situation, the Commission affirms again that the three fundamental issues in the urban problems of disadvantaged minorities are: employment, education and police-community relations. Accordingly, the Commission looks upon its recommendations in these three areas as the heart of its plea and the City's best hope.

As we have said earlier in this report, there is no immediate remedy for the problems of the Negro and other disadvantaged in our community. The problems are deep and the remedies are costly and will take time. However, through the implementation of the programs we propose, with the dedication we discuss, and with the leadership we call for from all, our Commission states without dissent, that the tragic violence that occurred during the six days of August will not be repeated.

Report of the National Advisory Commission on Civil Disorders—1968

This is the summary of the report of the Kerner Commission. The report, which has stirred much discussion, but little action, is the most important single national statement on the ethnic crisis of our time.

SUMMARY OF REPORT: INTRODUCTION

The summer of 1967 again brought racial disorders to American cities, and with them shock, fear and bewilderment to the nation.

The worse came during a two-week period in July, first in Newark and then in Detroit. Each set off a chain reaction in neighboring communities.

On July 28, 1967, the President of the United States established this Commission and directed us to answer three basic questions:

What happened?

Why did it happen?

What can be done to prevent it from happening again?

To respond to these questions, we have undertaken a broad range of studies and investigations. We have visited the riot cities; we have heard many witnesses; we have sought the counsel of experts across the country.

This is our basic conclusion: our nation is moving toward two societies, one black, one white—separate and unequal.

Reaction to last summer's disorders has quickened the movement and deepened the division. Discrimination and segregation have long permeated much of American life; they now threaten the future of every American.

This deepening racial division is not inevitable. The movement apart can be reversed. Choice is still possible. Our principal task is to define that choice and to press for a national resolution.

To pursue our present course will involve the continuing polarization of the American community and, ultimately, the destruction of basic democratic values.

The alternative is not blind repression or capitulation to lawlessness. It is the realization of common opportunities for all within a single society.

This alternative will require a commitment to national action—compassionate, massive and sustained, backed by the resources of the most powerful and the richest nation on this earth. From every American it will require new attitudes, new understanding, and, above all, new will.

The vital needs of the nation must be met; hard choices must be made, and, if necessary, new taxes enacted.

Violence cannot build a better society. Disruption and disorder nourish repression, not justice. They strike at the freedom of every citizen. The community cannot—it will not—tolerate coercion and mob rule.

Violence and destruction must be ended—in the streets of the ghetto and in the lives of people.

Segregation and poverty have created in the racial ghetto a destructive environment totally unknown to most white Americans.

What white Americans have never fully understood—but what the Negro can never forget—is that white society is deeply implicated in the ghetto. White institutions created it, white institutions maintain it, and white society condones it.

It is time now to turn with all the purpose at our command to the major unfinished business of this nation. It is time to adopt strategies for action that will produce quick and visible progress. It is time to make good the promises of American democracy to all citizens—urban and rural, white and black, Spanish-surname, American Indian, and every minority group.

Our recommendations embrace three basic principles:

> To mount programs on a scale equal to the dimension of the problems;
>
> To aim these programs for high impact in the immediate future in order to close the gap between promise and performance;
>
> To undertake new initiatives and experiments that can change the system of failure and frustration that now dominates the ghetto and weakens our society.

These programs will require unprecedented levels of funding and performance, but they neither probe deeper nor demand more than the problems which called them forth. There can be no higher priority for national action and no higher claim on the nation's conscience.

We issue this Report now, four months before the date called for by the President. Much remains that can be learned. Continued study is essential.

As Commissioners we have worked together with a sense of the greatest urgency and have sought to compose whatever differences among us. Some differences remain. But the gravity of the problem and the pressing need for action are too clear to allow further delay in the issuance of this Report.

Suggestions for Further Reading

HISTORY

The major texts in California history are John W. Caughey, *California* (2d ed., 1963), Andrew F. Rolle, *California* (2d ed., 1969) and Walton E. Bean, *California* (1968); the first is best on the earlier periods, the latter two on the modern, but none pays enough attention to ethnic factors. Theodora Kroeber, *Ishi* * (1965) is a haunting masterpiece; for a general view of discrimination against the Indian, Helen Hunt Jackson, *A Century of Dishonor* * (1881) is still worth reading. William T. Hagan, *American Indians* * (1961) is the best general volume. For the Mexican experience in California, Carey McWilliams, *North From Mexico* (1948) is probably the most useful despite its vintage; for a specialized account of the years following the American conquest see Leonard Pitt, *The Decline of the Californios* (1966). No good general account exists for the Chinese, but see Mary R. Coolidge, *Chinese Immigration* (1909) and Rose Hum Lee, *The Chinese in the United States* (1960). Much better, although they deal only with the 19th century are Gunther Barth, *Bitter Strength* (1964) and Elmer Sandmeyer, *The Anti-Chinese Movement in California* (1939). Jade Snow Wong, *Fifth Chinese Daughter* * (1950), is a charming and perceptive memoir of a modern San Franciscan. On the Japanese generally, the best account is Harry H. L. Kitano, *Japanese Americans: The Evolution of a Subculture* * (1969); for the reaction against them see Roger Daniels, *The Politics of Prejudice* * (1962). The relocation has been treated many times. The best book is Morton Grodzins, *Americans Betrayed* (1949); but see also the scholarly Jacobus ten Broek, *Prejudice, War and the Constitution* * (1954), and the popular Allan K. Bosworth, *America's Concentration Camps* * (1967). Monica Sone, *Nisei Daughter* (1953), is an account of a Seattle girlhood. There is no major work on the Negro in California (that this is still so is a major indictment of California historiography), although a few scholarly articles are beginning to appear. One of the best of these is Rudolph M. Lapp, "The Negro in Gold Rush California," *Journal of Negro History* (1964). The two best general histories of black Americans are the lengthy John Hope Franklin, *From Slavery to Freedom* * (3d ed., 1968), and the more brief August Meier and Elliott Rudwick, *From Plantation to Ghetto* * (1966).

PSYCHOLOGY-SOCIOLOGY AND RACE RELATIONS

The early work by the psychologist Gordon W. Allport, *The Nature of Prejudice*, Cambridge, Mass., Addison-Wesley Publishing Company, 1954, remains as a basic reading in the area. The much criticized but valuable psychoanalytic view of the prejudiced personality by T. W. Adorno, et al., *The Authoritarian Personality*, New York, Harper and Brothers, 1950, is another early view of the problems of prejudice. A recent book by William H. Grier and Price M. Cobbs, *Black Rage*, New York, Basic Books, Inc., 1968, illustrates psychological reactions of blacks to racism.

Michael Banton, *Race Relations*, London, Tavistock Publications, 1967, provides a thoughtful examination of race relations throughout the world. An earlier book by Brewton Berry, *Race and Ethnic Relations*, Boston, Houghton-Mifflin, 1958, is one among many books which summarizes the ethnic problems in our culture. The current Ethnic Groups in American Life Series (Milton M. Gordon, ed.) by Prentice-Hall provides a review of the actions and reactions of selected ethnic groups. Volumes include:

Sidney Goldstein and Calvin Goldscheider, *Jewish Americans: Three Generations in a Jewish Community*, Englewood Cliffs, N.J., Prentice-Hall, Inc., 1968.

Harry H. L. Kitano, *Japanese Americans: The Evolution of a Subculture*, Englewood Cliffs, N.J., Prentice-Hall, Inc., 1969.

Alphonso Pinkney, *Black Americans*, Englewood Cliffs, N.J., Prentice-Hall, Inc., 1969.

* An asterisk indicates paperback edition available.

Index

149